More Presbyterian Questions,
More Presbyterian Answers

Other Books by Donald K. McKim

The Church: Its Early Life
The Authority and Interpretation of the Bible:
An Historical Approach (with Jack B. Rogers)
The Authoritative Word: Essays on the Nature of Scripture (editor)
Readings in Calvin's Theology (editor)
What Christians Believe about the Bible
A Guide to Contemporary Hermeneutics:
Major Trends in Biblical Interpretation (editor)
How Karl Barth Changed My Mind (editor)
Ramism in William Perkins' Theology
Theological Turning Points: Major Issues in Christian Thought
Major Themes in the Reformed Tradition (editor)
Encyclopedia of the Reformed Faith (editor)
Kerygma: The Bible and Theology (4 volumes)
The Bible in Theology and Preaching
Westminster Dictionary of Theological Terms
God Never Forgets: Faith, Hope, and Alzheimer's Disease (editor)
Historical Handbook of Major Biblical Interpreters (editor)
Historical Dictionary of Reformed Churches
(with Robert Benedetto and Darrell L. Guder)
Calvin's Institutes: *Abridged Edition* (editor)
Introducing the Reformed Faith: Biblical Revelation,
Christian Tradition, Contemporary Significance
The Westminster Handbook to Reformed Theology (editor)
The Cambridge Companion to Martin Luther (editor)
Presbyterian Beliefs: A Brief Introduction
Presbyterian Questions, Presbyterian Answers
The Cambridge Companion to John Calvin (editor)
Calvin and the Bible (editor)
Historical Dictionary of Reformed Churches, 2nd ed.
(with Robert Benedetto)
Dictionary of Major Biblical Interpreters (editor)
Ever a Vision: A Brief History of Pittsburgh Theological Seminary,
1959-2009

More Presbyterian Questions, More Presbyterian Answers

Exploring Christian Faith

Donald K. McKim

Geneva Press
Louisville, Kentucky

Book design by Sharon Adams
Cover design by Night & Day Design

Library of Congress Cataloging-in-Publication Data

McKim, Donald K.
  More Presbyterian questions, more Presbyterian answers : exploring Christian faith / Donald K. McKim. — 1st ed.
      p. cm.
  Includes bibliographical references.
  ISBN 978-0-664-50308-6 (alk. paper)
  1. Presbyterian Church (U.S.A.)—Doctrines—Miscellanea. I. Title.
  BX8969.5.M37 2011
  230'.5137—dc22
                                                    2010033609

With gratitude and delight for dear friends
Jack and Diane Hodges
David and Linda McCreery
Jack and Pat Walchenbach

Contents

Preface

I have been very gratified by the reception of *Presbyterian Questions, Presbyterian Answers* (Geneva Press, 2003). Besides its use by individual readers—including seminary students—many churches turn to it for study groups, Sunday school classes, new members' classes, session meeting devotionals, and even some confirmation classes. This was my hope in writing the book, and I am most appreciative of those who have found it helpful in their journeys as Presbyterian Christians.

The 92 questions and answers in that book just scratched the surface of issues Presbyterians think about these days. Our Christian faith is a constant movement of faith seeking understanding, as St. Augustine said centuries ago. So it is natural—indeed, necessary—for us as Christians to probe questions of our faith and inquire about what our faith has to say about many things.

This book is an attempt to provide more answers for questions raised by Presbyterians. The answers are not full and extensive. They are not the only ones that can be given to these questions. But I hope they will provide a measure of satisfaction and will open doors to further reflection and discussion. A selection of resources to help in this quest is at the end of the volume.

Here are seven sections, each with seven or a multiple of seven questions. This is to encourage daily or weekly study for individuals, or some combination grouping of questions for groups to consider. Of course, the book can be read straight through or dipped into where and when one wants, for no special occasion.

As in the earlier book, I have written primarily for laity

and students who are interested in Presbyterian and Reformed theology. Presbyterians are part of the Reformed theological tradition, rooted in the sixteenth-century Reformation. We look to reformers such as John Calvin (1509–1564), Huldrych Zwingli (1484–1531), Heinrich Bullinger (1504–1575), and others as having provided helpful theological ways to understand God's revelation in Scripture.

But the Reformed tradition is a living and vital tradition. Wherever Reformed Christians went, they wrote statements of faith and catechisms, creedal expressions of what they believed about their faith. So questions and answers are part of the Reformed heritage. This impulse to articulate faith continues today.

The primary locus for this book is the Presbyterian Church (U.S.A.), which has been my lifelong home. The PC(USA) has a *Book of Confessions* that gives us guidance for belief. I have used the *Book of Confessions* as the only source for quotations here and have abbreviated it as *BC* in the text. Many other sources could have been tapped to expand the discussions. But I wanted to keep the answers as clear and focused as possible. While my context is the PC(USA), I believe there is much here that is applicable to other Presbyterian denominations and Reformed churches as well.

It has been wonderful to see other volumes of this sort emerge—for Methodists, Lutherans, and Baptists.* My ecumenical hope is that as greater theological understanding emerges among churches, we will recognize more clearly the strength and power of our unity in Jesus Christ, who is the head of the church (Col. 1:18). We need always to keep our parts of speech straight: We are "Presbyterian Christians," or "Lutheran" or "Methodist" Christians—the denomination is the adjective modifying the noun, "Christian," which is most important.

---

*See F. Belton Joyner Jr., *United Methodist Questions, United Methodist Answers: Exploring Christian Faith* (Louisville, KY: Westminster John Knox Press, 2007); Martin E. Marty, *Lutheran Questions, Lutheran Answers: Exploring Christian Faith* (Minneapolis: Augsburg, 2007); Bill J. Leonard, *Baptist Questions, Baptist Answers: Exploring Christian Faith* (Louisville, KY: Westminster John Knox Press, 2009). Marty hopes that "other Christian communions will pick up and trade on the example until there is a little shelf of question and answer books" (9).

So this book is for Presbyterian Christians interested in knowing more about Christian faith in its Presbyterian expression. I believe we participate best ecumenically when we understand our own theological heritage deeply. What follows is a modest offering to help Presbyterians and, I hope, the ecumenical church as well.

This book is also given to Presbyterians to encourage our reflection on theological questions and issues. There are treasures in our theological tradition to help us understand and live our Christian faith in this twenty-first-century world. I hope some of these treasures will be found here.

As always, I express gratitude for my family who blesses me. Since the first book was written, LindaJo and I have welcomed two wonderful daughters-in-law into our family. We rejoice for Stephen and Caroline and for Karl and Lauren.

It is a pleasure to dedicate this work to long-standing Presbyterian friends. Jack and Diane Hodges are two of our favorite people. David and Linda McCreery and Jack and Pat Walchenbach have been dear friends since our days at Pittsburgh Theological Seminary. For their lives and our friendship, I am deeply grateful.

Donald K. McKim
Germantown, Tennessee
Easter/Resurrection of the Lord
April 4, 2010

Ways to Use This Book

This book can be used in different ways.

Group study. This book has seven chapters, designed so groups in churches can study the book through a quarter of the church year. Each chapter has seven or a multiple of seven questions, which can be read by participants as a question and answer per day through a week. I hope this "easy dose" approach will encourage participants to read each chapter and then discuss it when the group gathers weekly. I imagine each question and answer will evoke further questions or perspectives, which can be discussed by the group as a whole. Of course, the time period for the group study can be extended into virtually any format. I trust that church groups of all types will find this book to be helpful.

Individual study. This book is also designed for individual study. I wrote it for those interested in knowing about Presbyterian beliefs. These may be persons who have a general interest, those who are considering membership in Presbyterian churches, those who are joining Presbyterian churches from other denominations, seminary students, or longtime Presbyterians who would like a focused look at our theological understandings. Individuals can use this book in nearly any way. I hope some will be encouraged to delve further into the many resources available so their Christian faith will be enhanced by greater understanding.

1

About Presbyterians

1. How do Presbyterians regard John Calvin (1509–1564)?

Presbyterians are always associated with John Calvin. This is a common connection made by people who are familiar with the Reformed and Presbyterian traditions as well as by those who have a less detailed picture.

John Calvin was a sixteenth-century French scholar who studied law and the liberal arts under leading Renaissance humanists. This training led him to be concerned with interpreting ancient texts, since the motto of the humanists was *Ad fontes*—"to the sources." Calvin became aligned with the concerns for reform of the Roman Catholic Church being led by Martin Luther (1484–1546) and soon gained notoriety for the first edition of his *Institutes of the Christian Religion* (1536), which he prepared to help people understand the Christian faith.

A series of events led Calvin to Geneva, where he began to teach and preach. A dispute with the authorities forced him to leave the city and become a pastor in Strassburg for three years. But Calvin returned to Geneva in 1541 and led the Protestant Reformation in the city until his death in 1564.

Calvin's teachings spread throughout Europe and into the New World. He and his followers became known as "Reformed" Christians, and they sought the reform of the church based on Scripture. His followers—sometimes called "Calvinists"—established churches based on Calvin's theological understandings.

This Reformed tradition is one branch of Protestantism, distinct from the Lutheran and Anabaptist traditions.

Calvin advocated a "presbyterian" form of church government, meaning a church governed by "presbyters" or "elders." Under such a system, local churches are governed by elders chosen by the congregation; churches in a region form a "presbytery." Larger groupings of churches form a "synod," and the churches together constitute a "General Assembly." Elders and ordained ministers of the Word and Sacrament have equal roles in church government.

Presbyterians look to Calvin as a guide for interpreting Scripture and gaining theological understandings. We do not "worship" Calvin; indeed, we recognize limitations in his own thoughts and formulations. But Calvin has been the major theological influence in the Reformed tradition, and his insights still provide guidance and nourishment for Presbyterian Christians today.

2. What is the *Book of Confessions*?

In 1967, the United Presbyterian Church in the United States of America (UPCUSA) voted to adopt a book of confessions as the doctrinal standard for the denomination. For over three hundred years, Presbyterians had looked primarily to the Westminster Confession of Faith (1647) as the single most important confession to express what Presbyterians believe. The *Book of Confessions* was a collection of ten documents from the early church to the present time that were other expressions of the Reformed faith to which Presbyterians adhere.

In the *Book of Confessions* when it was adopted in 1967 were two documents from the early church: the Nicene Creed and the Apostles' Creed. Also included were six documents from the Reformation era: the Scots Confession (1560), the Heidelberg Catechism (1563), the Second Helvetic Confession (1566), the Westminster Confession (1647), and the Westminster Shorter and Larger Catechisms. Two contemporary documents were the

Theological Declaration of Barmen (1934) and the Confession of 1967. Together, these confessions represented some of the breadth of the Reformed theological tradition, since they were expressions of Reformed Christians from different times and places.

In 1983, the United Presbyterian Church in the United States of America merged with the Presbyterian Church in the United States (PCUS) to heal a division that had occurred with the American Civil War. The new denomination became the Presbyterian Church in the United States of America, or PC(USA). In 1993, the denomination adopted A Brief Statement of Faith, which is now included in the *Book of Confessions*.

Confessions help us understand Scripture. They are expressions of what Reformed Christians believe is revealed in the Bible. They are theological formulations that are natural expressions of vibrant Christian beliefs. Reformed Christians have the urge to confess their faith!

Additional confessions of faith may be added to the *Book of Confessions* in future years. New confessions will use new terminology to address matters of vital Christian belief. The Reformed and Presbyterian tradition is a living, growing tradition. We seek always to hear God's word to us anew, even as we continue to confess the theological truths that have guided us to this day.

3. Do Presbyterians accept baptisms performed by other denominations?

Presbyterians are Presbyterian Christians. That is, "presbyterian" is our way of being Christians. There are many other denominations and bodies of Christian believers with whom Presbyterians share common beliefs. So we are first of all "Christians," and then "Presbyterians." We participate in the ecumenical church, which is the church of Jesus Christ spread throughout the world.

One of our common beliefs with all other Christians is our belief in the Trinity. We believe in "one God," whom we know as "three persons": Father, Son, and Holy Spirit. This core conviction is a basic Christian doctrine that the whole Christian church has held to since the early centuries.

Christian churches also administer baptism. Some churches baptize infants as well as adults. Some churches baptize only adults who confess their faith in Jesus Christ as Lord and Savior. Historically, Presbyterians have baptized both infants and adults.

Presbyterians accept the baptism of other denominations as being valid Christian baptisms if they were carried out with the "Trinitarian formula." This means that a baptism is considered valid if it was administered "in the name of the Father, the Son, and the Holy Spirit."

Despite differences in understanding about the nature of baptism among denominations, what matters most—and what unites Presbyterians and other Christians, as well as all Christians together—is our worship of and obedience to the "one God in three persons" we confess as Father, Son, and Holy Spirit. This common confession of who God is finds celebration in baptism. So Presbyterians recognize the theological validity of a baptism carried out in another church or denomination if that baptism was administered in the name of the triune God—Father, Son, and Holy Spirit.

For Presbyterians, baptism and the Lord's Supper are the two sacraments of the church. They unite church members with each other, and they unite us all in the church, with the God we know in Jesus Christ, by the power of the Holy Spirit. So accepting as valid the baptism of a person of another denominational body, carried out in the name of the triune God, is an expression of the ultimate unity of the Christian church.

4. What do Presbyterians believe about evangelism?

Evangelism is the sharing of the good news (gospel; Gr. *euangelion*) of Jesus Christ through a variety of means. This makes evangelism central to the life and ministry of Christian churches.

Presbyterians believe the church is to call people "to be reconciled to God and to one another" (*BC* 9.07) and by the power of the Holy Spirit has the courage "to witness among all peoples to Christ as Lord and Savior" (*BC* 10.4). We have the strongest impetus to proclaim the gospel of Jesus Christ in both "word" and "deed," by what we say and what we do, throughout the whole world.

Like the New Testament, we accent preaching as a primary way by which the message of God's love in Jesus Christ (John 3:16) is shared with the world. Through preaching, salvation can happen as people respond to Christ in faith (1 Cor. 1:18–21) by the power of the Holy Spirit (1 Cor. 12:3).

Presbyterians have emphasized God's election as God's graciously giving faith and salvation. We believe salvation is the gift of God's grace alone (Eph. 2:8–9). God has chosen us in Christ, according to God's "good pleasure" (Eph. 1:4–5), and we do not by our own will or power respond to the gospel. In the past, some people (called "hyper-Calvinists") said there was no need to evangelize or preach the gospel because if God chooses whom to save, God does not need preachers to preach! What they missed is the command of Christ to proclaim the gospel (Matt. 28:16–20) and the recognition that God uses preaching as the means by which the gospel story is proclaimed and, thus, believed.

Presbyterians today realize the message of Jesus Christ can be expressed in many different ways in addition to preaching and teaching. Evangelism is not an "end" in itself for churches. We do not try to gain church members to make ourselves "successful."

Instead, evangelism is our grateful response to the "good news" that God has come to us in Christ, that we can become a "new creation," and that we have been given the "ministry of reconciliation" to call people to "be reconciled to God" (2 Cor. 5:16–21).

5. Are Presbyterians "fundamentalists"?

The term "fundamentalism" came to prominence in the United States in the early part of the twentieth century, particularly in the

1920s during the "Fundamentalist-Modernist" controversy. At that time, many people believed the use of scientific methods to study the Bible (called "biblical criticism") along with advances in the sciences in many fields—and especially the theory of evolution—posed strong challenges to traditional Christianity. A series of twelve paperback books called *The Fundamentals: A Testimony of the Truth* was published between 1910 and 1915 to defend the claims of traditional Christian faith and to answer the charges of the movement known as "liberal theology," which held that many Christian claims should no longer be believed by modern persons in light of advancements in science and contemporary biblical studies. From these and a series of popular meetings, the "five points of fundamentalism" emerged. These doctrines were: the inerrancy of Scripture, the deity of Christ, the substitutionary atonement of Christ, Christ's bodily resurrection, and Christ's literal (premillennial) second coming.

The Fundamentalist-Modernist controversy included ongoing struggles in churches and within the larger American culture over these and related issues. The Presbyterian Church has gone through many debates that relate to the nature of Scripture and matters of biblical interpretation that were part of this larger conflict. Fundamentalists urged a literal reading of the Bible, including the early chapters of Genesis, and this led them to oppose evolution. Their view of biblical authority was that Scripture is an inerrant document, without any errors of any kind in all it affirms. This inevitably led to clashes with other theological views of the nature of the Bible and its appropriate interpretation.

In the latter part of the twentieth century, fundamentalism in the United States often became allied with conservative, political ideologies. Many denominations—most prominently, the Southern Baptist Convention—proclaim themselves fundamentalist.

The Presbyterian Church (U.S.A.) is not considered a fundamentalist denomination. We recognize varieties of ways of interpreting Scripture, and most members of the denomination do not see the Bible as "inerrant." We stress "the whole purpose of God" (Acts 20:27), rather than reducing Christian faith to a small number of doctrines.

6. Can Presbyterians believe in evolution?

Struggles over the theory of evolution have been frequent and often bitter. Since it was proposed by Charles Darwin in *The Descent of Man* (1871), Christians have taken different approaches on whether evolution is contrary to or compatible with Christian faith. This issue raises a larger one about the nature of the Bible. Christians who reject evolution do so because of what they believe the Bible is and how it should be interpreted. They believe the Bible is true and contains nothing contrary to truth in whatever it affirms in any area, including science and history. This belief in the inerrancy of the Bible is a hallmark of American fundamentalism. According to this view, the first chapters of Genesis, which describe creation, should be interpreted literally because they are presented as statements of fact. Since the Bible is the "Word of God," it must be true in all it affirms. A literal interpretation of the "days" in Genesis means rejecting evolution as a scientific theory since it does not match the biblical account.

Some Christians in the PC(USA) and other Presbyterian denominations hold to the inerrancy of Scripture and reject evolution on these grounds. But the majority of PC(USA) members view the Bible differently and in ways that uphold biblical authority while enabling them to be open to the findings of science.

One view is to recognize the Bible as God's Word and as a book with a theological purpose—to believe that it intends to answer "why" questions instead of "how" questions. Science tells us "how" things happen—how plants or animals or humans may evolve over time. The Bible, written by people in ancient cultures through the inspiration of the Holy Spirit, intends to tell us what we can find in no other source: why things are as they are and why God created the heavens and the earth.

In this way, we recognize that evolution, and other scientific findings, can provide important information within the realm of the "how," while theology and the Bible itself tell us in a unique and authoritative way "why" humans are created—by whatever scientific means God chose to use. Thus, the full authority of the Bible is upheld, and there is no inherent conflict between "science" and "faith," or between evolution and Christianity.

7. What do Presbyterians believe about the ecumenical movement?

The term "ecumenical" comes from the Greek word, *oikoumenē*, meaning "the inhabited world." The modern ecumenical movement is widespread and in various ways seeks to bring about unity among various Christian churches throughout the world. This occurs formally through organizations, as well as informally on local levels, with churches working cooperatively on projects of mission and ministry or in services of worship, learning, and fellowship.

Important features of the ecumenical movement have been concerns for cooperation among church bodies, desires for mutual understanding of different theological views, and respect for other Christians in recognition of our common witness to the gospel. Jesus prayed that his disciples "may all be one" (John 17:21). How that can and should be expressed by contemporary church bodies is an ongoing quest.

The most prominent expression of the formal ecumenical movement is the World Council of Churches (First Assembly, 1948). In the United States, the Federal Council of Churches of Christ in America (1908) and its successor organization, the National Council of Churches (1950), have played important roles.

In 1960, the Stated Clerk of the United Presbyterian Church, Eugene Carson Blake (1906–1985) preached a sermon in San Francisco in which he called for the union of major U.S. Protestant churches. This led to the formation COCU, the Consultation on Church Union, in 1962. In 1969, a formal merger proposal among the denominations was rejected. Since no structural union of the Protestant churches could occur, emphasis was put on "intercommunion" or "full communion." This meant the recognition of the validity of the rites and ministries of other denominations, while churches maintained their own identity. In 2002, COCU became Churches Uniting in Christ (CUIC), which recognizes intercommunion among full member churches.

Not all Presbyterian denominations in the United States have been part of these groups. But the PC(USA) and its predecessor denominations have participated in these formal ecumenical organizations. The PC(USA) encourages ecumenical cooperation on all levels for churches, recognizing that our impetus should be toward a greater expression of the theological unity the "whole household of God" (Eph. 2:19) has under Jesus Christ, the great head of the church (Col. 1:18).

2

Presbyterians and Others

8. What should be our attitudes toward other religions?

Our primary identity as Christians is that we are "in Christ" (Rom. 8:1). We are disciples of Jesus Christ, whom we believe is God's Messiah, the savior of the world (Phil. 3:20; Titus 3:6). This is who we are and who we will always be.

We live in a religiously pluralistic world along with persons of other historic faiths, such as Judaism, Islam, Hinduism, Confucianism, Shintoism, Taoism, and others. American Christians likely have friends or acquaintances from these faiths.

Presbyterians can hold an open attitude toward other religious faiths in the sense of being interested in them, learning from them, and being respectful of views and practices that differ from our own. This does not cause us to retreat from our Christian, and Presbyterian, beliefs. Rather, it recognizes the varieties of ways humans have expressed their desire to reach beyond themselves toward transcendent realities and toward ways of living in the world in relation to the environment and other people.

We can learn from other faiths. The Confession of 1967 says, "Christians find parallels between other religions and their own and must approach all religions with openness and respect. Repeatedly God has used the insight of non-Christians to challenge the church to renewal" (*BC* 9.42, inclusive language text; see http://pcusa .org/media/uploads/theologyandworship/pdfs/confess67.pdf for this text). As practitioners of various religions express their faith, especially on particular issues of significance and importance to the world community, we can consider their insights as a support and, at times, as a challenge to our Christian perspectives. Learning about other faiths in the midst of our pluralistic world is important. Church study groups as well as individuals should make this a priority.*

The Confession of 1967 also provides another dimension: "But the reconciling word of the gospel is God's judgment upon all forms of religion, including the Christian. The gift of God in Christ is for all. The church, therefore, is commissioned to carry the gospel to all whatever their religion may be and even when they profess none" (*BC* 9.42, inclusive language text). The church shares the Christian gospel with all persons throughout the world. Our learning from, respect for, and willingness to dialogue with other faiths does not diminish our primary commitment to the gospel of Jesus Christ, which proclaims God's love for the world (John 3:16).

9. What are some differences between Presbyterians and Roman Catholics?

Presbyterians are Protestants who during the sixteenth-century Protestant Reformation believed the prevailing Roman Catholic Church was teaching beliefs and carrying out practices that were not in accord with Scripture.

Since then, the Roman Catholic Church has changed greatly. With the Second Vatican Council (1962–1965), major new ways of thinking and expressing the Roman Catholic faith appeared. Theological dialogues between Roman Catholics and various groups, including Reformed Christians, have taken place.

Yet theological differences remain and historic issues are still important.

---

*An excellent resource for group and individual study is Howard R. Greenstein, Kendra G. Hotz, and John Kaltner, *What Do Our Neighbors Believe? Questions and Answers on Judaism, Christianity, and Islam* (Louisville, KY: Westminster John Knox Press, 2007). Here a Jewish rabbi, Christian theologian, and scholar of Islam provide succinct and accessible discussions of the perspectives of these three world faiths on the big questions of religion.

Authority. The Roman Catholic Church has regarded church tradition as a source of authority along with Scripture. The church interprets Scripture, through its magisterium and teaching offices. These interpretations establish church tradition. The church structure invests authority in the papacy, an office Presbyterians reject. For Presbyterians, Scripture is the authority for faith and life, with nothing else equal to it.

Salvation. A chief focus in the Reformation was salvation. Protestants believed Roman Catholicism taught we are saved by "faith"—interpreted as believing in the church's teachings—plus "good works," which are the actions the church prescribes a person to do. These together lead to salvation. Presbyterians believe we are saved by faith in Jesus Christ alone. Good works are an expression of faith but do not contribute to salvation.

Worship and sacraments. In the Roman Catholic Mass, Jesus Christ is believed to be resacrificed on the altar by the priest. The sacramental system of the Roman Church features seven sacraments: baptism, confirmation, Eucharist, penance, holy matrimony, holy orders, and anointing of the sick. These take one from the cradle to the grave. Being a good Catholic means believing what the church teaches and participating in the sacraments. Presbyterians believe Jesus Christ was sacrificed "once for all" (Heb. 7:27; cf. 9:28) and that there are only two sacraments: baptism and the Lord's Supper. Faith is trust in Jesus Christ, which engages our whole lives as we seek to be Christ's disciples in the church.

Presbyterians should seek all opportunities to discuss faith and participate ecumenically with Roman Catholic believers. Despite theological differences, our common unity is in Jesus Christ.

10. What are some differences between Presbyterians and Eastern Orthodox Christians?

Churches called "Eastern Orthodox" include Greek, Slavic, Antiochian or Syrian Orthodox, and other Orthodox churches. With Roman Catholicism and Protestantism, Orthodoxy is one of the three major divisions among Christian churches.

Orthodoxy developed from Christianity in the Greek-speaking Mediterranean area. It holds special regard for the first seven Ecumenical Councils of Christianity (AD 325–787), where the church's unity was expressed.

The split between "Eastern" and "Western" churches emerged over time, due to many political, cultural, and theological factors. Constantinople (Byzantium) had become the imperial capital of the eastern administrative unit of the Roman Empire, while Rome held that status in the west. Tensions between eastern and western branches of the church led to a formal break in 1054. The first point of contention involved the claims of the pope, the bishop of Rome, to be head of the church. Eastern churches recognized the pope as "first among equals" but were unwilling to grant him universal jurisdiction. The patriarch of Constantinople became the chief primate of the Eastern churches.

The second issue, that of the *filioque*, became a key theological dispute. This term, meaning "and the Son," refers to the phrase in the Nicene Creed that the Holy Spirit "proceeds from the Father and the Son" (*BC* 1.3). The pope had inserted the phrase "and the Son" into the Creed, and this was accepted by the Western churches. Both theologically and politically, the Eastern churches rejected this addition, claiming no single bishop could modify what an ecumenical council had established. Other differences related to the Eastern insistence on using leavened bread in the Lord's Supper and to aspects of worship, including the veneration of icons. The pope and the patriarch of Constantinople mutually excommunicated each other's churches, a situation not healed until the middle of the 1960s.

Presbyterians differ theologically with Eastern Orthodoxy on issues of authority in the church, the relation of Scripture and tradition, original sin, the roles of the divine and human in salvation, the use of images and icons in worship, and sacraments. The Orthodox do not share the Lord's Supper (Eucharist) with non-Orthodox church members, since the Eucharist is seen as a supreme expression of Christian unity and not a means toward which that unity is achieved.

11. What are some differences between Presbyterians and Episcopalians?

The Episcopal Church is part of the worldwide body of Anglican churches. Anglicanism considers itself "Protestant, yet Catholic," its origins in England representing a "middle way" between the traditional Roman Catholicism and the developing forms of Protestantism in the sixteenth and seventeenth centuries.

The Episcopal Church has an "episcopal" form of church government, meaning a structure that is hierarchical, with bishops playing a central role. Bishops are the heads of dioceses, and on the national level the church's chief officer is called the presiding bishop.

Theologically, the Thirty-nine Articles of Religion (1563) was a witness to Anglican viewpoints in relation to Roman Catholicism, Protestantism (Lutheranism and Calvinism), and Anabaptist movements. The Articles are generalized theological tenets that are not intended to be a creed. They have been variously interpreted through the years (for example, on the question of the presence of Christ in the Lord's Supper—article 28). That they have been open to different interpretations is reflective of the sixteenth-century context in which they were written, to encompass a broad "middle way" between Protestantism and Roman Catholicism. Thus the Episcopal Church itself encompasses a variety of theological positions and views of the Christian life. Some groups have broken away from the U.S. church over controversial issues and established links with Anglican churches in other places.

Traditional sources of authority for the church are Scripture, tradition, and reason. A place for religious experience is also commonly recognized. The Nicene and Apostles' creeds of the ancient church are looked to as normative expressions of faith.

Episcopal worship is highly liturgical, with variations in local churches. But the *Book of Common Prayer* (first book, 1549) binds the church together through liturgy that includes High Church, Low Church, and Broad Church services. The Eucharist is central to each worship service and with baptism is recognized as one of the two sacraments.

The largest denominations of Episcopalians and Presbyterians in the United States both ordain women to ministries and are socially active in orientation while participating ecumenically.

12. What are some differences between Presbyterians and Lutherans?

The Lutheran tradition and the Reformed tradition became the two major movements during the sixteenth-century Protestant Reformation. They are in accordance on many points and are opposed to a number of points of Roman Catholic theology. Some of these are the "bumper stickers" of the Reformation: Scripture alone, Christ alone, Grace alone, and Faith alone.

Both the Lutheran and Reformed traditions are confessional. They use confessions of faith as important guides for understanding Scripture. The Reformed tradition has never established one single confession or set of confessions as normative. But confessional authority in the Lutheran tradition is the *Book of Concord* (1580), which includes three early ecumenical creeds plus seven documents from Reformation times, including Luther's Large and Small Catechism and the Augsburg Confession (1530).

Central to Lutheranism is that humans cannot save themselves because of original sin but are saved by God's grace received through faith in Jesus Christ. We know of Christ through the Scriptures. Justification by faith expresses this main principle. Lutherans sharply distinguish between "law" and "gospel." The law condemns human righteousness in showing the impossibility of earning salvation, while the gospel proclaims salvation as God's free gift of grace to be received by faith.

A chief difference between Lutherans and the Reformed is the presence of Jesus Christ in the Lord's Supper. Lutherans teach the body of Christ is "in, with, and under" the form of the elements in the Supper (often called "consubstantiation"). The Reformed have several positions, the view of Calvin being that the presence of

Christ was real and spiritual in the Supper but not physical, since the body of Christ is in heaven. Those who receive the Supper in faith receive the benefits of Christ's work. This theological difference was a main stumbling block in bringing unity to the Protestant movement.

Lutheran churches have a highly liturgical form of worship, with hymns and preaching as central features. They have a hierarchical form of church government, with bishops as key officials.

Lutherans and Presbyterians find ways to work together in ecumenical and social ventures. They continue their dialogues on theological issues and on issues of ministry.

13. What are some differences between Presbyterians and Methodists?

In many places, it is hard to identify too many differences between the local Presbyterian and the local Methodist churches. Worship services are similar, common interests are many, and as people move back and forth to different communities they often are Presbyterian for a while, Methodist for a while, and then may switch back.

Historically, Methodism in the United States developed from the Methodist movement in England begun by John Wesley (1703–1791). Wesley was an Anglican priest who began open-air preaching from which began a number of small groups of Christians who met together to hold each other accountable for their Christian obedience while emphasizing discipleship and evangelism. In the United States, Methodism took shape as an independent denomination that—like other early denominations—split into a number of particular (Methodist) denominations in the coming years.

Theologically, Methodism looks to John Wesley and his brother Charles, who wrote thousands of hymns, and behind them to James Arminius (1560–1609), who questioned the views of Calvin, especially on the issue of election and predestination. Arminius emphasized the place of "free will," or human decision in one's conversion, instead of Calvin's views on salvation as a result of God's eternal election. The Arminian emphases continue in Methodist beliefs today, so that in worship services, "altar calls," which are opportunities to confess Christian faith, may be given.

Like Presbyterians, Methodists recognize baptism and the Lord's Supper as the church's two sacraments. They see authority in the church as emerging from Scripture, tradition, reason, and religious experience. The Presbyterian emphasis is more directly focused on Scripture alone.

Methodist church government is episcopal in structure, with bishops playing a major role. This differs from the Presbyterian system.

Historically, Methodists have been socially active. Their social principles have led Methodists to participate in social movements related to contemporary problems from education to temperance, and from gambling to issues of war, peace, and social justice. Methodists participate ecumenically on national and local levels.

Despite historic theological differences, some Presbyterians find themselves more closely allied on issues with some Methodists than with other Presbyterians, and vice versa.

14. What are some differences between Presbyterians and Baptists?

Baptists get their name because of their emphasis on baptism. Baptists believe infant baptism is not a valid baptism and that only "believer's baptism," or the baptism of those who have reached an age of accountability when they can confess their faith in Jesus Christ, is the only valid type of baptism. Baptism must be by immersion, not by any other means. These views are in contrast to Presbyterian theology, which sees both infant and adult baptism as valid forms of baptism. Presbyterians also recognize different modes of baptism, not insisting that baptism's validity depends on one particular way of administering the sacrament.

There are varieties in Baptist theology. Some Baptists

emphasize the place of human will and decision in conversion and theologically are aligned with the heritage that goes back to James Arminius (1560–1609), who was also a forerunner of Methodist theology. Other Baptists stress God's divine work of grace in conversion in ways that are more congenial with the teachings of John Calvin on election and predestination. These differing views are found throughout the many Baptist denominations.

Presbyterians are in the tradition of Calvin and also differ from Baptists in emphasizing the place of creeds and confessions of faith. Baptists do not invest creeds or confessional statements with any official status.

What unites Baptist churches is their congregational polity. Each individual congregation is autonomous and self-governing. Baptists have larger groups called "associations," but the primary unit of church government is the local church. By contrast, Presbyterians have a form of church government where the primary governing body is the presbytery.

Baptists do not see baptism and the Lord's Supper as sacraments, as do Presbyterians. For Baptists, these "ordinances" are purely symbolic and do not convey God's grace.

Historically, Baptists have stressed religious freedom and the separation of church and state. Baptists vary in the ways they interpret Scripture, many stressing reading the Bible in a literal sense. The majority of Baptists see themselves either as "fundamentalists" or "evangelicals," two terms that would not be major defining terms for the majority of Presbyterians.

3

Presbyterian Theology

15. What is God like?

We spend our whole lives trying to answer this question!

As Christians, we look to the Bible as the source for our knowledge of God. From beginning to end, the Bible is the story of a God who has created this world, guides this world, and enters into relationships with us as human beings so we can live lives focused on God's good purposes for us. These we know most clearly when we look at Jesus Christ, God's Son, our Lord and Savior.

Our church confessions provide many descriptions of who God is. The Second Helvetic Confession gives us two paragraphs: "God is One" and "God is Three" (*BC* 5.015; 5.016). These point to our belief in God as Trinity: one God in three persons—Father, Son, and Holy Spirit. This is our basic confession about God.

We also find that God is the creator of all things (*BC* 5.032), governs all things (5.029), and elects to save us in Jesus Christ (5.052). These are major biblical themes and key elements in knowing who God is.

But another theme makes all these descriptions of God even more real. The theme is faith, and faith means we can trust God.

God has established a relationship with us as human beings. The biblical story is that we sin and break this relationship, which was to be marked by human love, trust, and obedience to God (Gen. 1–3). But God has reached out to us in the person of Jesus Christ, who is "God with us" (Matt. 1:23). Through Jesus' death and resurrection we receive new life, as followers of Christ, who has delivered us "from death to life eternal" (*BC* 10.2).

God is a relational God whose nature and action is to love us: "God is love" (1 John 5:16). This love leads us to love others (1 John 5:7–21). Faith is our trust in this faithful God. In "everlasting love" (*BC* 10.3) God accepts us in Christ and calls us into the people of God (the church) to serve God and be sent into the world as God's "reconciling community" (*BC* 9.31).

16. Can we know God through nature?

When we look at a gorgeous sunset or a majestic ocean, or when we see twinkling stars at night, we may quote the psalmist: "The heavens are telling the glory of God; and the firmament proclaims his handiwork" (Ps. 19:1).

Some have argued that we can know God exists by observing and deducing from nature. If you probe the intricacies of nature, recognize its complexities, balances, and sheer greatness—it should convince you that God exists. This viewpoint is sometimes called "natural theology." A famous argument for the existence of God by William Paley (1743–1805) suggests the universe is like a watch, with many parts working in order and harmoniously. If you find a watch on a beach, you know there must be a "watchmaker" who has intelligently designed this complex, ordered, and purposeful watch. By analogy, the complex, ordered, and purposeful universe must also have a designer, a creator—so there must be a "God."

But the psalmist who saw the heavens proclaiming the glory of God already believed in God. The psalmist was part of a nation that believed in God as creator of all things and worshiped God, who had established a covenant relationship with the people of Israel.

There are logical objections to the so-called proofs for the existence of God. But whether they are logically valid or not, the important thing is to realize that neither reason nor the world around us can disclose the nature of the God who has created it all. This "creative force" or "watchmaker" may be brutal, or impersonal, or benevolent. Nature itself cannot tell us.

Christians, who already know the God we worship and serve is the "Maker of heavens and earth" (*BC* 1.1; 2.1), can proclaim that God is revealed in nature to the "eyes of faith." When we see nature, we see the work of God. Ultimately, we know God the creator is also God the redeemer, the God who in Jesus Christ is the "image of the invisible God" (Col. 1:15) and who "gave himself up for us" (Eph. 5:2).

17. What does "Father Almighty" mean in the Apostles' Creed?

We are used to this phrase from the first line of the Nicene and Apostles' creeds, followed by the next phrase, "Maker of heaven and earth" (*BC* 1.1; 2.1).

In early times, "Father" suggested God as the one who created all things. "Almighty" emphasized this and pointed to God's ultimate power and rule over everything that exists. A connected meaning that became prominent was the relational meaning. God as "Father" affirmed God as the one who has a parental relationship with humans; this is the one whom Jesus called "Abba, Father" (*BC* 10.3). In the early creeds themselves, "God the Father" is a member of the Trinity, in relation to God the Son (Jesus Christ) and the Holy Spirit.

We know theologically that the description of "Father Almighty" does not mean God is male. The purpose of the biblical term, recognizing the social contexts of the ancient times, was to point to the intimacy of the relationship—as between a parent and a child. The early creeds reflect this.

Key to the parental relationship of love between parent and child is also trust. We can trust the God who is the "Father Almighty." This takes many forms for us, but it is also a most comforting assurance.

This note is clear in the Heidelberg Catechism (1563). In

response to what this phrase means, part of the answer is: "I trust in him so completely that I have no doubt that he will provide me with all things necessary for body and soul" (*BC* 4.026). Our trust is in the God in whom Jesus himself trusted. This God is able to provide us with "all things necessary" for us because God loves us as a parent and is the "almighty" God who is sovereign over all things.

God as "almighty" does not mean God has a "bigger hammer" than anyone else and is sheer, naked power. God's "almightiness" is defined by God's nature as the one who loves us with the most tender love imaginable—parental love. This is the God in whom we can trust and whose provision for all our needs is utterly reliable.

18. What does it mean to say, "God is holy"?

A familiar Christian hymn, echoing Isaiah 6:3, is "Holy, Holy, Holy, Lord God Almighty." God is said to be "holy" not once but three times!

"Holy" is associated with God throughout the Bible, especially in the Old Testament. The psalmist said it directly: "For the Lord our God is holy" (Ps. 99:9). Israel knew from the start: "Who is like you, O Lord, among the gods? Who is like you, majestic in holiness, awesome in splendor, doing wonders?" (Exod. 15:11). God is "the Holy One of Israel" (Isa. 12:6). God stands over and beyond humans: "For I am God and no mortal, the Holy One in your midst" (Hos. 11:9).

This important way of describing God is reinforced by Jesus in the Lord's Prayer: "Hallowed [holy] be your name" (Matt. 6:9; "May your name be kept holy," TEV).

"Holy" means "sacred" or "set apart." God is holy as the One who is like no other, who is set apart from mortals, who is pure, and who has no fault or impurity. God is complete goodness and righteousness. This means that humans can never attain the status of "God" and can never, in ourselves, be perfect or unblemished.

Sin is what separates us from God. Compared to God, we have no standing or claim. We are impure. We worship and obey God in light of God's greatness and our sinfulness. God is awesome in the most basic sense of "inspiring awe."

The New Testament speaks of Christian believers being holy or pursuing holiness. We are to be holy, because God is holy (1 Pet. 1:14–16). The "saints" are those who are holy—and this is a designation for those in churches (1 Cor. 1:2; Phil. 1:2). We are called to be holy on the basis of our union with Jesus Christ by faith. We are set apart to be his disciples and followers. Christ imparts his holiness to us. Our growth in holiness is called "sanctification."

We honor God as holy as we worship and as we dedicate ourselves to following God's purposes for us and living according to God's will.

19. What does "Jesus Christ" mean?

"Jesus Christ" is a personal name and a title. We blend them together since it is Jesus Christ who is at the center of the Christian faith, the name "Christian" being an early designation for his followers (Acts 11:26).

"Jesus" goes back to the Latin *Iesus*, behind which stands the Hebrew name *Yeshoshuah* (Joshua), which means "Yahweh [God] is salvation" or "Yahweh has/will save." The name fits Jesus of Nazareth exactly! It takes on significance in the angel's announcement to Joseph prior to Jesus' birth: "You are to name him Jesus, for he will save his people from their sins" (Matt. 1:21). God saves us through Jesus.

"Christ" is a title. *Christos* in Greek means "anointed" and translates the Hebrew term *mashiah* ("messiah"). The people of Israel awaited the coming of the "anointed one," the "Messiah," the royal "son of David" through whom they hoped for deliverance and the ultimate establishment of God's reign of peace and justice in the messianic age (Isa.11:6; 49:1–6).

"Jesus Christ" became a proper name. Early Christians saw Jesus of Nazareth as God's messiah ("Christ") in whom God's Old Testament promises are fulfilled (Acts 2:31–36). He died to "save his people from their sins" (Matt. 1:21; cf. Rom. 5:8). He will ultimately reign as "King of kings and Lord of lords" (Rev. 19:16; cf. Phil. 2:5–11).

The development of the early church's views about who Jesus was and what he did became known as "Christology." It took several centuries for the church to establish a theological definition of who it understood Jesus Christ to be (Council of Chalcedon, AD 451). Our theological statements are guides to the directions in which we believe the Scriptures point. They seek to give more precise descriptions of what the Bible teaches.

Reformed theologians and our *Book of Confessions* give much attention to Jesus Christ. We stand in continuity with the views of the early church, captured in "A Brief Statement of Faith," which says, "We trust in Jesus Christ, fully human, fully God" (*BC* 10.2). We spend our lifetimes trying to understand and live out the implications of this confession.

20. What do we need to believe about Jesus Christ?

Jesus of Nazareth, called by Christians "Jesus Christ," has captivated people for centuries. His life and teachings have been studied, reflected on, and approached from many perspectives.

Presbyterians describe Jesus Christ in many ways. With all Christians, we acknowledge him as "Lord" and "Savior." This is the focus of our confession of faith when we join the Presbyterian Church. When asked, "Who is your Lord and Savior?" we respond, "Jesus Christ is my Lord and Savior."

We know Jesus Christ as our savior from sin. We witness to this faith to the whole world (*BC* 10.4, line 68). When the Heidelberg Catechism asks, "Why is the Son of God called JESUS, which means SAVIOR?" the answer is "Because he saves us from our sins, and because salvation is to be sought or found in no other" (*BC*

4.029). We believe Jesus Christ is "the unique and eternal Savior of the human race" (*BC* 5.077). No one else can solve the problem of sin, offer forgiveness, and restore our relationship with our creator, the loving God. We believe those joined to Jesus Christ by faith are "set right with God and commissioned to serve as God's reconciling community" (*BC* 9.10).

Our Savior is also our Lord. At the heart of New Testament confession is "Jesus is Lord" (Rom. 10:9). From this, the church developed a full theology and found ethical direction. "The Lordship of Christ" says all we are and all we do, as a church and as Christians, belongs to Jesus Christ and takes direction from him. Nothing is exempt! Jesus Christ is "Lord of all," of all our time, energy, devotion, resources—our whole selves, for all areas of life. There are no "other lords" (*BC* 8.15) to whom we belong. "Jesus Christ is Lord" is the most comprehensive of all claims. However we express it, we belong totally to God in Jesus Christ.

There are other ways of describing who Jesus is: liberator, model, man for others. But all need ultimately to point to Jesus' unique personhood and work and to proclaim him Savior and Lord.

21. What is covenant theology?

Sometimes Reformed or Presbyterian theology is called "covenant theology." Our tradition has particularly recognized "covenant" as a major biblical theme and a key way of understanding how God relates to humans through promises.

We see this in the Bible itself. It has two "testaments" (Lat. *testamentum*) or "covenants" (Gr. *diathēkē*). We speak of the "Old Testament" and the "New Testament," the latter of which is focused especially in Jesus Christ.

Presbyterians see God's covenant with Abraham and Sarah as a covenant of promise. Through them, God promises to bless "all the families of the earth" (Gen. 12:1–3) as they acknowledge

God in all they do. Other biblical covenants follow, such as the one with Moses at Sinai, where the people of Israel are called to live as God's covenant people (Exod. 20:1–2; Deut. 5:1–3). Israel's prophets remind the people of their covenant relationship when they sin (Jer. 11:1–5; Hos. 8:1ff.). Jeremiah looks to a "new covenant," in which God's law will be written on human hearts (Jer. 31:31–34).

Christians see all the covenants and promises of God as fulfilled in Jesus Christ. He is the "new covenant" who gave himself for us (Matt. 26:28; 1 Cor. 11:25). God's covenant is sealed in Christ, and as believers in Christ in the church, we are united with Christ by faith and receive all God's covenant promises in him (2 Cor. 1:20). The church is the covenant people of God. The sacraments of baptism and the Lord's Supper are expressions of God's covenant promises received in Jesus Christ. They are "holy signs and seals of the covenant of grace" (*BC* 6.149).

Presbyterians emphasize "covenant theology" as the link between the Old and New Testaments. God's covenants are God's relationships with us as the people of God, now centered in the "new covenant" in Jesus Christ. This is God's covenant of grace. God gives us a relationship we do not deserve, from sheer mercy! As the Westminster Confession puts it, "The principal acts of saving faith are accepting, receiving, and resting upon Christ alone for justification, sanctification, and eternal life, by virtue of the covenant of grace" (*BC* 6.079).

Covenant theology binds us together as God's people and "heirs according to the promise" (Gal. 3:29).

22. Why were the books we have in the Bible chosen to be in the Bible?

The books in the Bible make up what we call the canon of Scripture. "Canon" (Gr. *kanōn*) means a "measuring rod" or "measuring stick." The word came to mean a norm or standard by which one makes judgments or evaluations about things.

The Christian church eventually recognized a collection, or "canon," of books in the Old and New Testaments as constituting the Christian Bible (Gr. *biblia* ["books"]). The process of canonization and the establishment of what became the definitive collection of canonical books was long and complex. It took place over centuries and amid debates about what books should or should not be included in the canon of Scripture.

For the Old Testament, three main categories of writings became accepted as canon: the Law (Torah), Prophets, and Writings. After the Roman destruction of Jerusalem (AD 70), Jewish leaders wanted to have a "fixed" source of authoritative writings to tell the story of God's relationship with Israel. According to tradition, in AD 90, the Council of Jamnia established the list of writings that became the Old Testament or the Hebrew Scriptures.

For the New Testament, writings emerged after the death of Jesus, including letters by the apostle Paul and then several Gospels that told the story of the life of Jesus from distinctive perspectives. Other writings appeared as well. For the next three centuries, these writings circulated in Christian communities, and different lists of canonical books were proposed, in part to protect the church from various dangerous theological interpretations. An Easter letter by Bishop Athanasius in AD 367 is the first definitive listing of twenty-seven books, a list ratified thirty years later by the church council of Carthage.

While some books were controversial, the central core of books in both Testaments was never in doubt. The church accepted the Hebrew Scriptures as authoritative. New Testament writings—which had content emerging from the apostles and enriched the church's life, which were written by apostles and used in the church, and through which the whole church heard God's word—became part of the canon and continue to give us guidance for growth in our own lives today.*

---

*Two helpful resources are James E. Davison, *This Book We Call the Bible: A Study Guide for Adults* (Louisville, KY: Geneva Press, 2001), and John Barton, *How the Bible Came to Be* (Louisville, KY: Westminster John Knox Press, 1997).

23. What are the differences between the Protestant and Roman Catholic Bibles?

There are several major differences between the Bibles used by Roman Catholics and those used by Protestants, including Presbyterians.

The biggest difference is the number of books in each Bible. The Roman Catholic Bible consists of thirty-nine books of the Old Testament, twenty-seven books of the New Testament, plus seven additional books called the "Apocrypha" (Gr. *apokryphos* ["hidden"]; also called "Deuterocanonical Books"). The Apocrypha comes from the period between the Old Testament and the New Testament. These books were included in the Septuagint (LXX), the Greek translation of the Old Testament made for Jews living in Egypt approximately a century before the time of Jesus.

The Apocrypha consists of fifteen books or parts of books: 1 and 2 Esdras, Tobit, Judith, Additions to Esther, Wisdom of Solomon, Sirach, Baruch, Letter of Jeremiah, Song of the Three Youths (including the Prayer of Azariah), Susanna, Bel and the Dragon (this and the previous two known collectively as the Additions to Daniel), Prayer of Manasseh, 1 and 2 Maccabees.[*]

When St. Jerome translated the Bible into Latin in the fourth century (in an edition known as the Vulgate, which became the official Roman Catholic Bible), the Apocrypha was translated and became part of the Roman Catholic canon. These books were officially added to the Roman Catholic Bible by the Council of Trent (1546), after the Protestant Reformation.

The Protestant Bible consists of the thirty-nine books of the Old Testament and the twenty-seven books of the New Testament. At the time of the Reformation, the Protestant Reformers adopted the

---

[*]Greek Orthodox and other Orthodox churches also include 3 and 4 Maccabees and Psalm 151. The Psalms of Solomon are not typically included in the category of Apocrypha. See John J. Collins, "Introduction to the Apocrypha" in *Harper's Bible Commentary*, ed. James L. Mays (San Francisco: Harper & Row, 1988), 758–68.

books of the Jewish canon as the Old Testament canon and rejected the Apocrypha as books from which doctrine can be established. Another difference between Protestant and Roman Catholic Bibles is the translations. Only certain English translations have been given an official imprimatur by the Roman Catholic Church. These include the Jerusalem Bible (1966), the New American Bible (1970–1983), and the New Jerusalem Bible (1985). A wide variety of English translations are used by Protestants, including the New Revised Standard Version (NRSV), the New International Version (NIV), and the Contemporary English Version (CEV).

24. What do Presbyterians believe about the Virgin Mary?

Mary, the mother of Jesus (Matt. 1:16, 18–25; Luke 2:1–7), is often called the Virgin Mary (or Blessed Virgin Mary in the Roman Catholic tradition). The annunciation by the angel Gabriel indicated that she would bear a son and would name him Jesus (Luke 1:31; see also 1:26–56). After Jesus' early life, Mary is not prominent in the Gospels. But she is at the foot of the cross when Jesus is crucified (John 19:25).

Mary is identified as the "virgin Mary" in the Apostles' Creed (*BC* 2.2). The question of the virgin birth of Jesus has been disputed through the history of the church. Not all Presbyterians believe in a literal virgin birth.

Presbyterians can refer to Mary as "God-bearer" (Gr. *theotokos*), a term from the early church to describe Mary as "the mother of God." This affirms the divinity of Jesus Christ, who was born of a woman (Gal. 4:4) and, as the church confessed, had two natures, divine and human. Since the human Jesus is also the divine Jesus, one can speak of Mary as "God-bearer."

Another disputed question has been the "perpetual virginity" of Mary. Did Mary remain a virgin for the rest of her life, especially in light of references to Jesus' "brothers" and "sisters" (Matt. 13:55–56)? Roman Catholicism and Eastern Orthodox Christianity have affirmed Mary as "ever virgin," a phrase that is also found in the

Second Helvetic Confession (*BC* 5.064), though this has not been the dominant viewpoint of later Protestantism.

Roman Catholicism teaches the immaculate conception of Mary, meaning Mary was exempt from original sin from the time of her conception in her mother's womb. In 1950, Pope Pius XII took matters a step further by declaring the "assumption" of Mary to be Roman Catholic dogma. This dogma teaches that Mary was assumed in body and soul directly to heaven.

As Protestants, Presbyterians have rejected the immaculate conception and bodily assumption of Mary. For us, Mary has traditionally been seen as a model for Christians of one who was completely obedient to God's will. Her commitment, as expressed in Luke 1:38, is an example for us: "Here am I, the servant of the Lord; let it be with me according to your word."

25. What is idolatry?

Idolatry has been a concern in the Reformed and Presbyterian tradition since it is so basic to human life under the power of sin.

The Ten Commandments forbid the making of an idol, as a visible form before which people bow down and worship (Exod. 20:4–6). The story of the golden calf worshiped by the people of Israel was a graphic example of what this could be (see Exod. 32:1–10) and its sinfulness in the eyes of God.

But the prohibition against the worship of idols (Exod. 20:5) means more than physical actions only. It concerns the attitude of the heart, the source from which worship emerges. The apostle Paul explains the origin of idolatry as the rejection of God's revelation where worship of God the creator is replaced by worship of a creature (Rom. 1:18–23). This is insidious sin and wickedness before God.

In both the Old Testament and the New Testament, idolatry means putting anything in the place that God alone should occupy as the focus for one's allegiance and obedience in life (see Col. 3:5). This is clear from the Heidelberg Catechism, which to the question "What is idolatry?" answers, "It is to imagine or possess something in which to put one's trust in place of or beside the one true God who has revealed himself in his Word" (*BC* 4.095). We don't think much about idolatry today and less so if we confine it in our minds to bowing to an image, icon, or some artifact. Idolatry is much more pervasive, rooted as it is in our deepest dispositions. When we rely on anything other than God, we worship an idol. When we trust our own abilities, wealth, status, achievements—whatever—then idolatry is alive. We may set goals for life or seek fulfillments in various ways. But when these become ends in themselves or such a primary focus of our attention and trust and energy that we are not first seeking God's will and worshiping God, then we sin against God and worship idols of our own making. Idolatry puts oneself at the center of life.

26. Are all sins equal?

In Roman Catholic theology, there is a distinction between "mortal" and "venial" sins. A mortal sin can cause ultimate separation from God, eternal death. A venial sin does not cause such drastic consequences, but it is still evil because it turns one's heart away from God.

Our Reformed and Presbyterian tradition has not gone along with this distinction. At the core, all sins are sins against God that deserve God's judgment (Rom. 6:23). We are sinners by nature, and "all have sinned and fall short of the glory of God" (Rom. 3:23). We are sinful in our origins as humans, what theologians call "original sin." Our actual sins arise from this condition. The Second Helvetic Confession says of original sin:

> We acknowledge that all other sins which arise from it are called and truly are sins, no matter by what name they may be called, whether mortal, venial or that which is said to be the sin against the Holy Spirit which is never forgiven (Mark 3:29; 1 John 5:16). We also confess that sins are not equal; although they

arise from the same fountain of corruption and unbelief, some are more serious than others. (*BC* 5.039)

We realize there are gradations of sin in that the effects or consequences of some sins are worse than others. Jesus pointed to this when he spoke about anger (Matt. 5:21–22). But sin is still sin, and all sin needs to be confessed and forgiven by God. We should never look at our sins and say, "Well, they could have been worse!" This would be to excuse ourselves for our sinful actions. We try to evade responsibility and live with alibis. We need to confess all sins, no matter their magnitude, and repent, trusting in God's forgiveness (1 John 1:9).

The Westminster Confession says, "As there is no sin so small but it deserves damnation; so there is no sin so great that it can bring damnation upon those who truly repent" (*BC* 6.084). Our focus should never be to "justify" ourselves in our sin. It is always to recognize the seriousness of sin, seek forgiveness, and turn from sin to walk in the light of Christ (1 John 1:7).

27. What happens when we confess our sins?

Presbyterians realize the importance confessing our sins and asking God's forgiveness.

Our services of worship include a confession of sin in which we acknowledge our sin individually and corporately. In our corporate confession, we confess not only our own sins but also the sins of humanity of which we are a part. We recognize our solidarity as part of the human family and realize sinful actions affect not only the sinner but others as well.

Our confession of personal sin, in worship and in private, is the entryway to God's forgiveness. Like the psalmist, we acknowledge our sin to God (Ps. 51:1). In this confession we find forgiveness (Ps. 32:5). As Christians, we find that "if we confess our sins, he who is faithful and just will forgive us our sins and cleanse us from all unrighteousness" (1 John 1:9). This forgiveness comes to us in Jesus Christ (Acts 13:38–39).

Theologically, God forgives our sin on the basis of Christ's death on the cross, the benefits of which we as Christians receive by faith. The Westminster Larger Catechism puts it in technical terms. In the petition from the Lord's Prayer to "forgive us our debts," the catechism says, we "pray for ourselves and others, that God of his free grace would, through the obedience and satisfaction of Christ apprehended and applied by faith, acquit us both from the guilt and punishment of sin" (*BC* 7.304). Put more simply in the Barmen Confession, "Jesus Christ is God's assurance of the forgiveness of all our sins" (*BC* 8.14). When we confess our sin, we have the promise of God's loving forgiveness, shown to us in Jesus Christ.

We confess our sins because we are sorry for them. "Repentance" is our contrition and then our turning to walk in "newness of life" (Rom. 6:4), away from sin. Repentance is God's gift to us (*BC* 5.094). Forgiveness liberates us from sin's power. As the old rhyme puts it:

> 'Tis not enough to say
> I'm sorry, and repent,
> And then go on from day to day
> Just as I always went.

Our confession of sin means a new life ahead!

28. What are different ways of understanding salvation?

Christian salvation is the restoration of our relationship, as sinners, with the God who loves us and sent Jesus Christ to die for us (John 3:16; Rom. 5:8). Presbyterians recognize that "our whole salvation is rooted in the one sacrifice of Christ offered for us on the cross" (*BC* 4.067).

Biblically and theologically, we recognize that many different images and descriptions can be used to describe the meaning of Jesus' death on the cross as the means of salvation (see *BC* 9.09). These varieties can lead us to a rich and full view of salvation. This is important because it points us to the reality that salvation "finds" us, in all the different situations of life. Whatever our need, salvation provides a way of understanding how God in Jesus Christ has reached out to meet our need.

Some important theological ways to understand salvation are these:

Liberation. By his death, Jesus liberates us from all enslaving powers. We are free people in Jesus Christ. We speak of "addiction" to various forces or of being "slaves of sin" (Rom. 6:20). Only Jesus Christ provides the power and new life to liberate us from corporate and personal enslaving powers. We are "called to freedom" (Gal. 5:13), and "for freedom Christ has set us free" (Gal. 5:1).

Forgiveness. The death and resurrection of Jesus Christ brings forgiveness of sin (Eph. 1:7) and our justification before God (Rom. 4:25). The power of our past is not definitive for us. It need not stand against us. Whatever we have done can be forgiven by God (Ps. 32:1; Isa. 6:7). New life can be ours in Christ (Luke 15:11–32; 2 Cor. 5:17).

Peace. Our salvation through Jesus Christ is the gift of peace (Rom. 5:1). Christ himself is our peace (Eph. 2:14), the content of the "gospel of peace" (Eph. 6:15). This was promised by the angels at the birth of Jesus (Luke 2:14) and has now become a reality for all who believe. This is the message we proclaim (Acts 10:36). Our relationship with God is secure in Jesus Christ. No threat, harm, or fear can "separate us from the love of God in Christ Jesus our Lord" (Rom. 8:39).

29. Are babies who die, saved?

This question has been speculated upon by the church since the early centuries. Normally, we believe the way to salvation comes through confession of Jesus Christ as Lord and Savior, which leads to baptism as a sign of incorporation into the church, as the family or "elect" of God. Presbyterian churches, along with other churches, practice infant baptism, through which the children of Christian believers are received into the church, later to confess their personal faith in Christ when they are older, in the rite of confirmation. But the question arises about the salvation of infants who die before they are baptized. In the Roman Catholic tradition, baptism is considered essential for salvation. It is seen as washing away the guilt of original sin, which, if it were not cleansed, would prevent one from entering heaven. So if there is no baptism, the argument goes, then infants who die cannot enter heaven. The theory of the "limbo of infants" (Lat. *limbus infantium*) has been endorsed by the church to say that unbaptized infants experience the utmost of natural happiness in a state of "limbo." Contemporary Roman Catholic theology entrusts unbaptized infants to the "mercy of God" in the hope (but not the sure knowledge) that there is a way of salvation for them.

Presbyterians do not believe infant baptism (or baptism of adults) is necessary for salvation. Baptism is a sign of the salvation we have received by the grace and election of God. Unbaptized infants who die are commended to God's grace. In 1903, a Declaratory Statement was added to the Westminster Confession that says, "We believe that all dying in infancy are included in the election of grace, and are regenerated and saved by Christ through the Spirit, who works when and where and how he pleases" (*BC* 6.193).

This statement is the authoritative interpretation of a phrase in the original confession (1647) that referred to "elect infants" (*BC* 6.066) and led to speculation there may be "nonelect infants." But the church's declarative interpretation comforts us in the confidence of God's loving embrace.

30. What is the atonement?

"Atonement" is an English word invented by William Tyndale (c. 1494–1536) in his translation of the Bible into English. Tyndale realized there was no English term that directly translated the key Old Testament concept that God and humans can be united through the forgiveness of sins in the rituals of the "Day of Atonement" (Heb. *Yom Kippur*). Tyndale coined "atonement" to describe the New Testament's affirmation that through the death of Jesus Christ, human sin can be forgiven and that God and humanity can be reconciled. Both aspects are present in Christ's death. The atonement of the death of Jesus Christ is a central part of Christian faith (Rom. 5:8; Eph. 1:7; Col. 1:20).

The Christian church has never said there is only one way to understand how we are saved through Christ's atoning death. Many theories of atonement have sought to explain how the death of Christ saves. Some describe a change in the sinner's status before God based on Christ involving God's looking at the sinner in a new way. Other views emphasize a change in the person of the sinner.

Unless one denies the efficacy of the death of Christ, one cannot be a heretic on the doctrine of the atonement! The Confession of 1967 says,

> God's reconciling act in Jesus Christ is a mystery which the Scriptures describe in various ways. It is called the sacrifice of a lamb, a shepherd's life given for his sheep, atonement by a priest; again it is ransom of a slave, payment of debt, vicarious satisfaction of a legal penalty, and victory over the powers of evil. These are expressions of a truth which remains beyond the reach of all theory in the depths of God's love for humankind. They reveal the gravity, cost, and sure achievement of God's reconciling work. (*BC* 9.09)

No one expression can capture the fullness of what the atonement means. A wise theologian said the reason there was darkness when Jesus hung on the cross (Mark 15:33) was so that no one could go home and say they had seen it all! There is more to the death of Christ than we can ever know.

31. What is faith?

Faith is a central component of the Christian life, the mark of the people of God in the Old and New Testaments and in the history of the church. Biblically, "faith is the assurance of things hoped for, the conviction of things not seen" (Heb. 11:1). Faith moves us beyond our own minds and emotions, to assurance of a reality that can come in no other way. People of faith have looked to God as the source and object of their faith, and to Jesus Christ as the one through whom God is known and in whom God's promises are fulfilled (2 Cor. 1:20). Faith comes by God's grace through the work of the Holy Spirit.

The Heidelberg Catechism gives a very practical definition of faith:

> Q. 21. What is true faith?
>
> A. It is not only a certain knowledge by which I accept as true all that God has revealed to us in his Word, but also a wholehearted trust which the Holy Spirit creates in me through the gospel, that, not only to others, but to me also God has given the forgiveness of sins, everlasting righteousness and salvation, out of sheer grace solely for the sake of Christ's saving work. (*BC* 4.021)

Faith is the means by which we recognize and come to love Jesus Christ as our Lord and Savior and to trust him for salvation. This faith is "a pure gift of God" by the Holy Spirit (*BC* 5.113; cf. Eph. 2:8–9). We believe not because we are "smart" or "worthy," but purely by God's gracious election in giving us what we do not deserve. Christians have a faith "they have not of themselves" but that "is the gift of God" (*BC* 6.069). The "principal acts of saving faith," the Westminster Confession says, "are accepting, receiving, and resting upon Christ alone for justification, sanctification, and eternal life" (*BC* 6.079; cf. 6.078).

We are saved by "faith alone," but it is never a faith that *is* alone. Our faith in Christ leads us to serve Christ and serve others. Faith is active in love (Gal. 5:6), and "faith by itself, if it has no works, is dead" (Jas. 2:17).

32. What is "regeneration"?

"Regeneration" is a theological term used to describe the work of God's Holy Spirit in which those elected by God and called to be Christians have "a new heart and a new spirit created in them" (*BC* 6.075).

A principal New Testament text is Titus 3:5, which says we are saved "not because of any works of righteousness that we had done, but according to his mercy, through the water of rebirth and renewal by the Holy Spirit." In the King James Version (1611), the phrase is "by the washing of regeneration, and renewing of the Holy Ghost." This is the biblical idea that God creates new life. God makes us a "new creation" in Christ Jesus (2 Cor. 5:17). God's Holy Spirit revolutionizes our lives, as Jesus told Nicodemus, by making us be "born from above" (John 3:3, 7). The Spirit brings life (John 6:63).

When this action of God's Spirit occurs, our lives are revolutionized. We are "reborn," becoming new persons in Christ. Through the Spirit, our sin is forgiven and we know we are "children of God" (John 1:12; Rom. 8:14), adopted into God's family (Rom. 8:15–17), now to live and love and serve God in Jesus Christ as "Christians." "Faith" is our first act as new people; regenerated by God, we confess our belief and trust in Jesus Christ as our Lord and Savior (1 John 5:1).

Presbyterians have seen regeneration as preceding faith. Our salvation is fully by God's grace alone, not by any human works we do (Eph. 2:8–9). God has "made us alive" in Christ by the Holy Spirit (Eph. 2:5). In Reformed thought, regeneration is the expression of God's election. God has elected us or chosen to save us by God's sheer grace and mercy, not by any worth or merit from us. God saves us without our cooperation, or power, or faith.

This is why regeneration is an important term. It reminds us our salvation is purely the work of God, without any human part. When we become new persons by regeneration, we respond in faith and confess, "My Lord and my God!" (John 20:28).

33. Must we have a "born-again" experience to be saved?

"Born again" is associated with American evangelicalism and has become a familiar part of our religious vocabulary.

It has been part of Christian experience to recount a "conversion experience" through which one came to a decision of faith in Jesus

Christ as Savior. This reorients life so that one passes from death to life in Christ (Rom. 5:21; 1 John 3:14). Most dramatically, the conversion of Saul of Taurus, who became the apostle Paul (Acts 9:1–9), marks the power of such experiences.

Jesus told Nicodemus he must be "born from above" (John 3:3, 7), which can also be translated "born again" (KJV). Christian experience recognizes we are "born anew . . . through the living and enduring word of God" (1 Pet. 1:23).

It is possible to know the date and time when one "became a Christian." John Wesley (1703–1791), the founder of Methodism, recounted how he went to a meeting of Moravians in London. When he heard a reading from Martin Luther's preface to his commentary on Romans, at about "a quarter to nine," Wesley felt his heart "strangely warmed." This revolutionized Wesley's life.

While the reality of passing from death to life in Christ and having faith in Christ as our Lord and Savior is true and marks Christian faith, it is not necessary to know the date and time when this event occurred or when we became conscious of it.

In Presbyterian theology, we believe God gives us the gift of faith by God's gracious election through the Holy Spirit, who can work whenever and however God desires (John 3:8). That we are "born from above" means our salvation is the work of God. Our experience of it may be such that if we are born into a Christian home, we may grow to adulthood, never remembering a time when we were not a Christian. Most important is to be able to say we love Jesus Christ as our Lord and Savior. When or how this reality comes varies with each person.

So we do not have to be able to point to a definite experience of being born again to be genuine Christians.

34. Can I be saved by "being good" or obeying the Ten Commandments?

If everyone everywhere obeyed the Ten Commandments, the world would be a different place. The problem is that none of us can obey the Ten Commandments perfectly; indeed, because of human sin, we do not desire to follow the Ten Commandments. We prefer to live life our own way rather than God's way.

This is why our salvation has to come not from our own efforts—since we can never live good lives by ourselves—but from God's gracious, electing grace, which is freely given to us. This is expressed in the most famous verse in the Bible: "For God so loved the world that he gave his only Son, so that everyone who believes in him may not perish but may have eternal life" (John 3:16).

Our salvation comes by God's grace through faith as the gift God gives us by the Holy Spirit. The slogan of the sixteenth-century Protestant reformers Luther and Calvin was "Grace alone; Faith alone." As sinful people, we cannot obey the Ten Commandments or live good lives by ourselves. We need a savior from sin, who is Jesus Christ, who can do for us what we cannot do for ourselves. God gives us salvation in Christ Jesus, who is the only one who ever obeyed God's commandments perfectly.

Once we are saved from the power of sin, we will seek to live good lives, or lives in obedience to God's will, as expressed in the Ten Commandments. Our good works do not save us; they are an expression of the salvation that has been freely given to us.

Our good works, according to the Scots Confession, are of two kinds: "the one is done to the honor of God, the other to the profit of our neighbor" (BC 3.14). As Luther put it, good works do not make a person good, but a good person will do good works.

We rejoice that our salvation does not depend on our keeping God's law, but that it is the free gift of God in Jesus Christ (Rom. 6:23; Eph. 2:8).

35. Why do we say, "He descended into hell," in the Apostles' Creed?

Some people have been known to stand silent when the congregation comes to "he descended into hell" while reciting the Apostles' Creed. Maybe they don't want to say "hell." Maybe they don't believe this or know what it means.

This phrase did not come into most versions of the Apostles'

Creed until sometime between the sixth and eighth centuries. By the beginning of the ninth century it was part of the official version of the creed. Many early Christians believed it, but it became interpreted in different ways.

This phrase clearly indicates the true death of Jesus. It comes right after "crucified, dead, and buried." Jesus was fully human, and this included his genuine death.

One view is that Jesus descended to the realm of the dead ("Sheol" in traditional Jewish belief) to preach to those who had lived before Jesus' time and were imprisoned there. First Peter 3:18–20 speaks of Jesus' preaching to "the spirits in prison" (v. 19). By the Middle Ages, a popular view was that Jesus preached to give the people who lived before his time the opportunity to receive salvation.

Another interpretation is that in his death, Jesus won victory over the powers of evil and descended into the realm of the death, the seat of evil, to bring forth the souls who were captive there. Ephesians 4:8–10 (quoting Ps. 68:18) speaks of Jesus ascending and also descending to the "lower parts of the earth."

Another view, favored by John Calvin and found in the Heidelberg Catechism, is the spiritual view. We do not interpret the descent literally but rather find it to mean that "in my severest tribulations I may be assured that Christ my Lord has redeemed me from hellish anxieties and torment by the unspeakable anguish, pains, and terrors which he suffered in his soul both on the cross and before" (*BC* 4.044). This makes the phrase meaningful to us in an ongoing way. It assures us of Christ's presence with us to redeem us—even in the deepest agonies of life.

36. What is the communion of saints?

We move through this little phrase from the Apostles' Creed, scarcely realizing it is breathtaking!

The phrase has been understood in various ways. This is because there have been seven grammatical translations of the Latin *sanctorum communio*. Several views are most important.

In the Middle Ages, a sacramental view of "participation in holy things" was a primary way of understanding the term. This reflected the Roman Catholic emphasis on the sacraments as vital for salvation.

A second perspective refers the phrase to the present-day church. "Saints" is a New Testament term for Christians in the church (1 Cor. 1:2). In the church we have "communion"—fellowship—with other Christian believers. So the phrase emphasizes the importance of the "union of saints," who participate in the mutual love and service of believers in the body of Christ. We share a common union in Christ. As the Heidelberg Catechism puts it, we understand "first, that believers one and all, as partakers of the Lord Christ, and all his treasures and gifts, shall share in one fellowship. Second, that each one ought to know that he is obliged to use his gifts freely and with joy for the benefit and welfare of other members" (*BC* 4.055).

A further emphasis in the Reformed tradition is to extend the image to the whole host of God's people from the beginning, throughout history—past, present, and future. We are surrounded by "so great a cloud of witnesses" (Heb. 12:1) that today we share in the same promises and blessings of God as did those who went before us and as will those who will come after us. So to confess the "communion of saints" gives us a comprehensive vision of the church of all ages and places us in the fellowship of that great company. This is the breathtaking view of who we are as part of the whole people of God in all ages.

Whatever view we take reminds us of the communal nature of our faith and that the realities of God's church are greater than we can know.

37. What is the meaning of Maundy Thursday?

"Maundy Thursday" designates the Thursday before Easter. Most Presbyterian churches have an evening service on Maundy Thursday that includes the celebration of the Lord's Supper. This marks the traditional day on which Jesus instituted the Lord's Supper during his last meal with his disciples and before Good Friday, when Jesus died on the cross.

The term "maundy" is from the Latin word *mandatum*, meaning "mandate" or "commandment." In the Gospel of John there is no mention of the sharing of the bread and the wine in the meal of Jesus and his disciples. What John has instead is Jesus' washing his disciples' feet (John 13:5ff.) and giving them a command: "If I, your Lord and Teacher, have washed your feet, you also ought to wash one another's feet" (John 13:14).

In traditional church liturgies of the washing of the feet, the first antiphon or responsive music features the Latin term *mandatum novum*, or "new commandment." This is from Jesus' command at the end of his washing the feet of his disciples when he said, "I give you a new commandment, that you love one another" (John 13:34).

Jesus' command for his disciples to love one another is repeated in the Gospel of John (15:12, 17) and is in force through the rest of the New Testament (e.g., Rom. 12:10; 13:8; Gal. 5:13; 1 John 3:18; 4:7).

Jesus' footwashing enacts his whole posture through his ministry of service and love for others. The footwashing is a visual parable. It is a complement to Jesus' institution of the Lord's Supper, in which the bread and the wine are visible expressions of his body and blood given for his disciples and for the world (e.g., Mark 14:22–25; 1 Cor. 11:23–26).

As the context for the church's celebration of the Lord's Supper and Jesus' footwashing, ending with the command to love others, Maundy Thursday is a powerful time of receiving and giving. We receive the benefits of Christ's body and blood, given for us in salvation. We give ourselves as Christ's disciples to live out his love for the world through our love for others.

38. What is the meaning of Good Friday?

Good Friday is the Friday before Easter, when the church remembers Jesus' death on the cross.

Jesus' death is central to Christian faith. The church sees Jesus' death as the basis of salvation, the reconciliation of God and humanity; only in this way can the Friday be called "good." It resulted in breaking the power of sin and in new life for those who believe (2 Cor. 5:16–21). "Christ crucified" (see 1 Cor. 2:2) shows God's wisdom and power (1 Cor. 1:18–31) in the person of God's Son, who "gave himself for us that he might redeem us from all iniquity" (Titus 2:14).

The Brief Statement of Faith encapsulates the meaning of Good Friday:

> Jesus was crucified,
> suffering the depths of human pain
> and giving his life for the sins of the world. (*BC* 10.2)

On Good Friday, the church confesses that Jesus Christ was a human being like us while also being the Son of God whose death can atone for the sins of the world. He was "fully human, fully God" (*BC* 10.2). Both Jesus' humanity and divinity are important.

As "fully human," one of us, Jesus entered completely into our human experience, except for sin. His identification means he stands in solidarity with us, in all our suffering, grief, and sin. When we sing, "What a friend we have in Jesus, All our sins and griefs to bear," we have the comfort and confidence that Jesus stands *with* us and *for* us.

As "fully God," the second person of the Trinity, Jesus' death has the power to bring forgiveness and reconciliation. In his ministry, Jesus showed divine power in what he did. Jesus was God's power in person, the power of suffering love. Through this love, our sin is forgiven and reconciliation becomes a reality.

Good Friday is a day of inexhaustible depth. Jesus' death reaches us where we are and provides for our greatest needs. The power of Jesus' death keeps reaching out for us in ways that evoke our response to profound love. As Isaac Watts put it, "Love so amazing, so divine, Demands my soul, my life, my all."

39. What is the meaning of Easter?

Easter is not about candy, or springtime, or bunnies. Easter is about the resurrection of Jesus Christ.

The resurrection of Christ was the message of the earliest Christians. New Testament affirmations link Christ's death for our sins with his being "raised on the third day" (1 Cor. 15:3–4; Rom. 1:3–4). This is echoed in the church's early creeds—"The third day he rose again from the dead" (Apostles' Creed, *BC* 2.2; cf. Nicene Creed, *BC* 1.2)—as well as the contemporary Brief Statement of Faith:

> God raised this Jesus from the dead,
> vindicating his sinless life,
> breaking the power of sin and evil,
> delivering us from death to life eternal (*BC* 10.2).

The cross and resurrection go together. Without the cross, the resurrection would not bring its full message. Without the resurrection, the cross would not carry the fullness of its power. It is God who raised Jesus from the dead (Acts 13:30). Jesus was raised "for our justification" (Rom. 4:25). The cross is empty; the risen Christ reigns!

In the resurrection, we see the life Jesus lived is the true life. It is the kind of life that is ultimately victorious. The way of service and love is vindicated. At the end of his great resurrection chapter, Paul assures us that "in the Lord your labor is not in vain" (1 Cor. 15:58). Our lives as disciples of Jesus have meaning since Jesus is raised.

The power of sin and evil is broken in Jesus' resurrection. Those are not the "last words" in life. The power of God is stronger than all opposition. The resurrection previews God's ultimate reign, when all earthly kingdoms "become the kingdom of our Lord" (Rev. 11:15). We work for justice and peace now, knowing God will reign (1 Cor. 15:25).

In Jesus' resurrection, the promise of eternal life is now realized

(1 John 2:25), and we have a preview of eternity. As justified by grace, this hope of eternal life is ours forever (Titus 3:7).

40. What is the ascension, and what do Presbyterians believe about it?

At Christmas we have pageants, at Easter, lilies. What do we have for Ascension Day?

The ascension of Jesus Christ is an important theological event. But it passes quickly in the Apostles' Creed: "He ascended into heaven, and sitteth on the right hand of God the Father Almighty" (*BC* 2.2). The church recognizes Ascension Day, forty days after Easter. But we don't do much to celebrate it.

Three biblical passages describe Jesus' ascension, which is viewed only by his disciples (Mark 16:19–20; Luke 24:50–53; Acts 1:9–11). Mark indicates Jesus was received into heaven and was seated "at the right hand of God," a place of honor and authority (Mark 16:29; see Ps. 110:1).

In Luke, Jesus' disciples see him "carried up into heaven" and return to Jerusalem "with great joy" (Luke 24:51–52, a reminder of the angels singing at Jesus' birth in Luke 2:10).

The detailed account in Acts indicates a forty-day period between resurrection and ascension, marked by Jesus' appearances and teachings (Acts 1:3). The disciples saw Jesus lifted up, "and a cloud took him out of their sight" (1:9). "Cloud" refers to God's glory and presence (Exod. 40:34). Now Jesus is in God's immediate presence. After the ascension, Jesus' earthly appearances ended. The descent of the Holy Spirit at Pentecost is next, fulfilling Jesus' promise of the Spirit's coming (Acts 1:4–5).

What does it all mean? Did Jesus literally ascend? Did he go up into the hills and vanish? We don't know. But no matter, three important truths stand out.

First, Christ opens the way to the heavenly kingdom. Now heaven is open to us since Jesus Christ is already there. Now we are seated with God "in the heavenly places in Christ Jesus" (Eph. 2:6). What joy!

Second, Christ is our advocate and intercessor. Christ acts on our behalf at the "right hand of God," forgiving and interceding. Christ is "for us" (Rom. 8:34; Heb. 7:25). What comfort!

Third, Christ provides his power for us. Christ defeated sin and death. Now we have Christ's power, by the Holy Spirit. Christ is our constant companion. His power ultimately reigns (1 Cor. 15:25). What confidence!

So celebrate ascension—everyday!

41. What is the "holy catholic church"?

Our primary experience with "church" is with the congregation we are part of, week after week, year after year. When we say the Apostles' Creed, we confess our belief in the "holy, catholic church." But what we know best is the "not-so-holy local church"!

It's sometimes hard for us to look beyond our own experience and to think of church in the big picture. This is what the phrase from the creed points us toward.

Holy. If we think of "holy" in terms of moral purity, it will be tough to say we believe in a holy church. The church is a community of sinners in need of God's forgiveness. The church is precisely where God's forgiveness is experienced.

The church is holy in the sense that it is "set apart." We are a people set apart to love and serve God in this world, by the power of the Holy Spirit. This phrase in the creed comes in the section on the Holy Spirit. The church is where we experience the presence and the power of the Holy Spirit so we as the people of God can carry out God's purposes in the world.

Catholic. This word sticks in the craws of some Protestants, who think it means "Roman Catholic"—as in the Roman Catholic Church. It doesn't. The term means "universal" or "extending through the whole world." The Christian church is worldwide. It is the whole family of God, everywhere.

"Catholic" also means "according to the whole." That is, people from all over are part of the church and contribute to the church. We are "many bodies in one bloodstream." There is diversity to the church, with every Christian sharing gifts with the whole body of Christ. We can therefore rejoice in the kaleidoscopic nature of the Christian church, finding the whole body enriched by the gifts of the parts contributing to the whole.

This phrase lifts us beyond ourselves and our own local congregations. We are part of the people of God, in all its diversity and in every place.

42. What do we mean by "eternal life"?

Sometimes called "everlasting life" (Dan. 12:2, and often in the King James Version), "eternal life" is both a present and a future reality.

We think most naturally of "eternal life" meaning a life that is eternal in duration—that is, it never ends. Jesus speaks of this in the parable of the Sheep and the Goats (Matt. 25:31–46). Two destinies await: the righteous go on to eternal life, and the others go on to eternal punishment (25:46). This life in the coming age is sought by the rich man who asked Jesus, "What must I do to inherit eternal life?" (Mark 10:17; Luke 10:25). This life is promised to those who believe in Jesus, as he told Nicodemus. These, says Jesus, "will not perish" (John 3:16; cf. 1 Tim. 1:16).

Eternal life in the future is eternity in the presence of the eternal God, images of which are found especially in the book of Revelation (see Rev. 21 and 22).

But "eternal life" is more. Eternal life is a quality of life that begins now. This is strong in the Gospel of John. In Jesus Christ is "life" (John 1:4; 5:26), and his words are spirit and life (6:63). Belief in him is the way by which true life is received (5:24; 20:31). This life, received by Jesus' disciples (20:22), comes to us by the Spirit (6:63) and is Jesus himself, experienced in baptism (3:5; cf. 7:37–39) and nourished by the Lord's Supper (6:51–58).

This life in Christ by the Spirit cannot be destroyed by death

(8:51–52; 11:26). Eternal life is the life of the age to come, given to believers in Christ right here, right now. This is what scholars call "realized eschatology"—the promises of the future, made real in the present. Eternal life is to know God and Jesus Christ (17:3). We receive eternal life now, as we abide in Jesus Christ as branches to the vine (15:5).

We anticipate a glorious future, even as we experience a life that is "eternal" in quality—the kind of life God intends, in our daily experience as we live now in Jesus Christ.

4

Christian Life

43. What does it mean to say we are "in Christ"?

"In Christ" (Gr. *en Christo*) is shorthand for saying we are Christians. Presbyterians, with other believers, recognize we live in a relationship with Jesus Christ, who is our Lord and Savior. This is a relationship of faith. We believe in Christ, trust Christ, and live as his disciples. We live the Christian life, by the power of God's Holy Spirit within us and among us, in "union with Christ." This union, by faith, is the closest bond we can know. It is so real and strong we can say we are "in Christ."

This phrase was a favorite of the apostle Paul. Paul used this term very often (e.g., 1 Cor. 3:1; Col. 1:2). Some say it was the heart of his faith. It indicates the transformation of our lives from people who live "in sin" (Ps. 51:5; Rom. 6:1), to those who now live "in Christ." This dramatic transformation frees us from the power of the law—which judges us when we do not live up to its commands—and enables us to live by the Spirit, "free from the law of sin and death," as people "in Christ" (Rom. 8:1–2). This is so radical Paul can write, "So if anyone is in Christ, there is a new creation: everything old has passed away; see, everything has become new!" (2 Cor. 5:17).

We are elected "in Christ" (*BC* 5.053; 5.054), have faith "in Christ" (*BC* 3.16; 5.110), and find our union with Christ expressed in baptism (7.276) and the Lord's Supper (7.281). Being "in Christ" comprehends the whole of Christian life. In short, "life in Christ is life eternal" (*BC* 9.26).

We would never describe our lives as "in St. Francis" or "in John Calvin." Both are dead and gone. But we do say we are "in Christ." Jesus Christ is living and present with us. Our union with Christ by faith is the deepest reality we know. We are "in Christ" and Christ is "in us." As Paul put it, "I have been crucified with Christ; and it is no longer I who live, but it is Christ who lives in me" (Gal. 2:20).

44. How can "all things work together for good"?

Paul's statement in Romans 8:28 is one of the most comforting promises of Scripture, but it sounds too good to be true. Because it does, we may wonder if it *can* be true.

Theologically, this verse relates to providence, an important doctrine for Presbyterians. This is our conviction that God is at work in the world, sustaining us, cooperating with us, and guiding our lives and human history itself through God's desired purposes. God does not create us and step back, leaving us alone. God—through Jesus Christ and the Holy Spirit—is actively involved in our lives, working to accomplish God's intentions for us.

This is the great trust we can have as Christian believers. The promise from Paul is that "all things work together for good for those who love God, who are called according to his purpose" (Rom. 8:28). God is at work in all things, including the adversities of life, to accomplish God's good purposes for us. This is a promise to give us confidence and comfort.

It is not that everything that happens to us is good in itself. We live through too much heartache and difficulty to believe that to be true. Instead, the promise is that all the events and circumstances of our lives are joined in such a way that overall, in their totality, God's good purposes are worked out.

How this can happen is a mystery to us. We remember the experience of Joseph, whose brothers sold him into slavery in Egypt. At the end, after Joseph recognized his brothers years later, he forgave them and said, "Even though you intended to do harm to me, God intended it for good" (Gen. 50:20). God was able to use Joseph's difficulties and troubles to carry out what God wanted to do in and through the life of Joseph.

This promise gives us comfort, not because it promises we will be exempt from problems or sufferings or tragedies or any of the dangers life presents. Our comfort is in God's good love for us and in God's guiding purposes, which can work in and through us to accomplish God's will.

45. What helps do we have for living the Christian life?

When young people were confirmed as members of a Presbyterian church, they used to be asked, "Do you promise to make diligent use of the means of grace?" When this question was asked of me, at eleven years old, I wondered what the "means of grace" were.

Since then, it has become somewhat clearer to me. "Means of grace" are helps God gives us to enable us to live the Christian life. Presbyterians emphasize the Holy Spirit as the one who enables us to "grow in the grace and knowledge of our Lord and Savior Jesus Christ" (2 Pet. 3:18). Theologically, we call this "sanctification." The Holy Spirit gives us means of grace through which our lives of faith in the church can be expressed.

What are these? Certainly they include the Scriptures, prayer, worship, and the sacraments. Each of these is a way by which we can grow in grace and knowledge. These provide the "rhythms" for our lives in the church, the things we do year in and year out that are ways God's grace and love take hold within and among us to enlarge our vision of what it means to be disciples of Jesus Christ.

We can recognize the church itself as the context in which these helps for the Christian life are carried out. There is no solitary Christianity—thank God! God gives us sisters and brothers in faith.

Christian action—working for peace and justice, as well as acting in Christian service to others—is a way the Spirit helps us grow as Christians. The church as communion of saints ensures that our life of faith is a corporate life as we "bear one another's burdens" (Gal. 6:2).

In addition, there are the people God gives us along our way, who are themselves means of grace. They minister to us; in them, we sense the presence of God's love. These are those to whom we can say, "I thank my God every time I remember you" (Phil. 1:3).

46. What does it mean to "take up our cross" and follow Jesus?

We associate the cross not only with Jesus' death but also with the call to discipleship he issued: "If any want to become my followers, let them deny themselves and take up their cross and follow me" (Mark 8:34). Luke's version says, "take up their cross daily and follow me" (Luke 9:23). Some see this as the ethical center of Jesus' teachings.

This call to discipleship clearly involves our self-denial, the "death" of our own ambitions. This was Dietrich Bonhoeffer's emphasis in his famous statement that when Christ calls a person to be a disciple, he calls that person to come and die. In the starkest terms, we are faced with saying no to ourselves and yes to following Jesus.

This following is a taking up of our cross. It means being willing to follow Jesus even to the extreme point of death or willingly to embrace what the cross means for our lives.

These aspects point us to the struggles of the Christian life, the ways in which being a follower of Jesus goes against our natural inclinations and impulses. We surely see this in "the way of Jesus Christ" who asks us to treat other people, even enemies, with love instead of hate (John 13:34; Luke 6:27), to pursue paths of peace (Luke 19:42), to seek forgiveness instead of revenge (Luke 6:37), to be merciful (Luke 6:36), to give to those who ask (Luke 6:30).

All this is possible only if we love Jesus Christ above all else and seek first God's reign, which Jesus himself embodied (Matt. 6:33). Self-denial and bearing the cross mean valuing Jesus and the reign of God as the true "treasure" in our lives, beyond all other interests. As Jesus says in Matthew 6:21, "Where your treasure is, there your heart will be also."

Both individually as Christians and corporately as the church we hear Jesus Christ, whom "we have to trust and obey in life and in death" and who is "God's mighty claim upon our whole life" (*BC* 8.11; 8.14). Above all, we follow him.

47. What do Presbyterians do during Lent?

Lent is the forty-day period before Easter. The term comes from the Middle English *lente*, meaning "spring," and originally from the Old English *lengten*, meaning "to lengthen"—referring to daylight. Lent begins with Ash Wednesday and in the early church was a time to prepare candidates for baptism. Later it became a period of fasting and penitence for the baptized, in preparation for Easter.

Presbyterians observe Lent in various ways. In some churches there are special Lenten worship services or fellowship times, often midweek. Sometimes churches in the same community join for common worship services. Liturgically, special prayers, or liturgical forms, or sanctuary decorations may be used. Preaching during Lent is usually marked by themes of repentance, self-examination, discipleship, and a focus on the disciplines of the Christian life.

Perhaps two directions indicate what Presbyterians do during Lent.

First, Presbyterians can "give up" something for Lent. This has been a traditional posture in the church catholic. During Lent, as a sign of devotion and discipleship, some Christians let go of something important. Fasting, as self-denial, has been part of Lenten disciplines in some traditions. For Presbyterians, the purpose of giving up something for Lent is to have more time to spend in some form of devotion, such as prayer or Scripture reading, or an appropriate activity. The point is to focus ourselves more directly on our faith. The season of Lent can provide opportunities for this to happen if we change our lifestyles with this purpose in mind. Second, Presbyterians can "take on" something for Lent, adding rather than subtracting. What can I take on as an additional dimension of my Christian life during this time? It may be more devotional activities, but also additional forms of service to the church and the world. Volunteer work, visitation of others, meeting human needs in tangible forms—all can be ways of enhancing one's Christian discipleship during Lent by adding actions to our lives. The purpose is to do these things consciously and as an explicit way of affirming, witnessing to, and enacting our faith.

48. Is it a sin to express doubt or to question our faith?

Doubt, in various forms, is part of the experience of most Christians. For some, doubt is so severe that questions in various forms may threaten completely to destroy their Christian faith. For others, questions arise over time or on specific issues. These are reflected on, discussed, and can often be resolved in satisfying ways. It is natural to have questions on issues of faith that are deeply important to us. But it is helpful to keep our doubts in perspective, as much as possible, so they do not seem overwhelming or paralyzing to the essential elements of our faith—intellectually, emotionally, and spiritually.

Doubt can be a positive factor in our Christian lives. Some wish Christian faith were like the old folk song "Home on the Range," where "never is heard a discouraging word, and the skies are not cloudy all day." They wish their faith would never have to ride the curved back of a question mark!

A basic Presbyterian conviction, from our Reformed heritage and going back to the fourth-century theologian Augustine, is that as Christians we live by "faith seeking understanding." Our Christian faith seeks to reach out and understand as much as possible. "Doubt" is part of this process. The issues, questions, and perplexities that arise are ones with which our faith ought to deal. Not all things are neatly resolved; there are always ongoing questions. But the process of doubt can be a positive factor when doubts lead us to examine our faith more fully and deeply and when our doubts can lead us to a deeper appreciation of faith and to new understandings.

So doubt or questions about our faith should not be regarded as sinful; they are means God can use to bring our faith to new places. Sometimes one gets to the point of beginning to "doubt one's doubts." There are some questions that are mysteries of faith to which fully satisfying intellectual explanations cannot seem to be given. But in the process of faith seeking understanding, our questions can lead us to a stronger integrity in coming to know what we believe.

49. Is it a sin to be tempted?

The Lord's Prayer includes a request for God to "lead us not into temptation" (Matt. 6:13). Some current English translations use "test" (REB) or "time of trial" (NRSV) to translate the Greek term earlier translated as "temptation."

Temptation in the sense of incitement to do evil (as in earlier usage) and "temptation" in the sense of testing or trial are both dimensions of this term in the Old and New Testaments. When we are tempted, we have choices: which way to follow, which decision to make. Some choices can be seen as in accord with the will of God, while others will run in a counter direction—away from or against what we may know God desires for us.

The situations represent a test or trial, and our responses have consequences. When we yield to temptation and act in ways against God's purposes, we face the prospects of guilt and estrangement (Ps. 51). When we recognize our actions as sin, we seek God's forgiveness and a restoration to God's favor (Ps. 51:12).

Temptations come in many forms, often subtle and alluring rather than clear and blatant. The Scriptures promise we will not be tested beyond our strength (1 Cor. 10:13) and will be "blessed" when we endure temptation (Jas. 1:12). God does not tempt us. Rather, temptation is through "one's own desire"—desire that can lead directly to sin (Jas. 1:13–14).

Theologians often tell us it is not a sin to be tempted; the sin is giving in to the temptation and turning away from God's will. As the old saying puts it, "You cannot prevent the birds from flying over your head, but you can certainly keep them from building a nest in your hair."

Temptations will come, yet we have resources on which to draw. We can seek God's ways in the midst of them through prayer and the advice of others. We can turn to Jesus Christ, who himself was tempted as we are (Heb. 4:15; Matt. 4:1–11) and who understands our needs. We can seek Christ's aid, since "he is able to help those who are being tested" (Heb. 2:14).

50. What is Christian freedom?

Christian freedom describes our new life in Jesus Christ. Jesus promised his disciples, "You will know the truth, and the truth will make you free" (John 11:32), and that "if the Son makes you free, you will be free indeed" (John 11:36). In Christ, we are "freed from sin" (Rom. 6:7, 18) and from "the law of sin and of death" (Rom. 8:2).

Our salvation, which releases us "from the guilt of sin," gives us "free access to God" (*BC* 6.108), making us free persons serving God in Jesus Christ, by the power of the Holy Spirit. So our Christian lives in the church are not regulated by rules to follow to overcome our pasts or gain a relationship with God (Gal. 5:1–15). What a relief!

Our freedom in Christ is not an excuse for self-indulgence. Instead, we are free to love others (Gal. 5:13). This is our liberty in Christ. Love expresses our Christian freedom. We are not only free *from* (the power of sin), but we are free *to* (love others). Love is the motive for Christian living and the expression of our union with Christ, since, as Paul writes, "the whole law is summed up in a single commandment, 'You shall love your neighbor as yourself'" (Gal. 5:15).

We live as free people, "servants of God," using our freedom not as "a pretext for evil" (1 Pet. 2:16). As we experience the Spirit of the Lord, we find freedom (2 Cor. 3:17). The Spirit "sets us free to accept ourselves and to love God and neighbor," while binding us together "with all believers in the one body of Christ, the Church" (*BC* 10.4).

Practically for Presbyterians, this means the church pursues the purposes of God's love in the freedom of the gospel of Jesus Christ, whom we "trust and obey in life and in death" (*BC* 8.11). It means that as Christ's disciples you and I seek the purposes of love for others. We are open to the unexpected and marvelous ways the Spirit leads us in the freedom of loving service.

Our freedom in Christ will ultimately lead us to the "freedom of the glory of the children of God" (Rom. 8:21). What a joy!

51. How do we know we are saved?

The Barmen Declaration affirms that "Jesus Christ is God's assurance of the forgiveness of all our sins" (*BC* 8.14). This is our assurance of salvation. To know we are saved, we ask ourselves, "Do I believe in Jesus Christ?"

More fully, the Westminster Confession affirms that those who "truly believe in the Lord Jesus, and love him in sincerity, endeavoring to walk in all good conscience before him, may in this life be certainly assured that they are in a state of grace, and may rejoice in the hope of the glory of God: which hope shall never make them ashamed" (*BC* 6.097).

Assurance of salvation has been a concern of many for fear of self-delusion. What if I think I believe in Christ but really do not? There are all kinds of psychological reasons that can be proposed to make us question the sincerity of our belief.

But the important emphasis for Presbyterians is that our assurance of salvation is not based on us and our strength of belief—

"upon a fallible hope." Rather, it is based on "an infallible assurance of faith, founded upon the divine truth of the promises of salvation" and the work of the Spirit of God within us (*BC* 6.097; Rom. 8:16–17). It is God's Spirit who testifies within us that we are the children of God whose sin is forgiven and that we have received "peace with God through our Lord Jesus Christ" (Rom. 5:1–2). In other words, God assures us of our salvation by the Holy Spirit. Assurance comes from God.

At times, as "true believers" our assurance of salvation may be "shaken, diminished, and intermitted," as the Westminster Confession says (*BC* 6.100). Yet we are never left "destitute of that seed of God, and life of faith, that love of Christ and the brethren, that sincerity of heart and conscience of duty, out of which, by the operation of the Spirit, this assurance may in due time be revived" (*BC* 6.100).

We can know we are saved by the Spirit's work within us, giving us a certain knowledge that we believe in Christ, love Christ, and are seeking to live in obedience to God's will.

52. Must I belong to a church to be saved?

For Presbyterians, salvation rests on God's gracious love in Jesus Christ, a gift we receive by faith alone. By the work of the Holy Spirit we receive the gift of faith, through which we love and trust Jesus Christ for salvation.

While this happens within our individual lives and experience, the nature of faith in Christ is to move us into relationship with other Christian believers. The church is the fellowship of faith, the people of God. The church is the means God uses to carry out God's purposes in this world. The church's one foundation is Jesus Christ (Eph. 2:20), and as members of the body of Christ (1 Cor. 12:27), we who are reconciled to God are "sent into the world as God's reconciling community" (*BC* 9.31, inclusive language text; see http://pcusa.org/media/uploads/theologyandworship/pdfs/confess67.pdf for this text).

So the church is crucial for our Christian lives. It is not an option, to take or leave, like what kinds of accessories to get for your new car. The church is essential. There is no "Lone Ranger Christianity" in which we try to live the Christian life all by ourselves.

Being a member of a local church is the normal way our Christian faith is expressed. Presbyterians would not say we must belong to a church in order to be saved. This would turn church membership into a "work" or a "condition" for salvation that we must fulfill. Instead, we are saved solely by God's grace through faith—not by any works of our own, of any kind (Eph. 2:8–9).

In some cases, we can imagine a person becoming a Christian, receiving the gift of salvation, and then because of some circumstances not being able to become part of the visible body of Christ in the church. Illness, death, or something else may intervene.

But in the usual course of our lives, we heed the biblical instruction that we not neglect "to meet together, as is the habit of some" (Heb. 10:25). We express the salvation we receive by participating fully with other believers in the church community, where our new lives in Christ take shape and are lived out.

53. Is our material prosperity a sign of God's favor?

No. Proponents of the "prosperity gospel" say that if one is prospering in the world, it is because God is blessing this person for being godly. An incentive to living a "godly" life, therefore, is so material blessings will come and we will experience the practical (including financial) benefits of Christian faith.

The example of Job in the Old Testament, a man who was upright and blameless in God's sight (Job 1:1) but suffered losses of possessions and family, is a counterexample to the view that living a godly life alone ensures prosperity.

Despite this, many popular media preachers claim one can attribute material success and prosperity to God. Relatedly, they say this is what God wants to give and that our prayers should be for these things. The example of Jabez (1 Chr. 4:9–10) is cited as a prayer for blessing and material prosperity that God answered positively.

But this kind of view treats God as "neutral energy," which we tune in, just as we tune in radio waves around us. If you simply desire hard enough and pray, you can get anything you want from God.

Jesus encouraged his followers to pray. But his own life was a test for our prayers. Our prayers should reflect our desire to live in accord with God's will, a will we see most clearly in Jesus. Some would say Jesus came to help us reach our goals. But it is more biblical to recognize that Jesus came to help us set our goals. Our prayers should look to his life and teachings as their primary focus. Jesus' emphasis was on love, forgiveness, justice, and peace rather than seeking material prosperity for ourselves. Jesus' admonitions not to set our hearts on the treasures of life (Matt. 6:19–21) and to beware of the corrosive danger of riches (Luke 18:22–25) are important warnings we always need to hear.

Many Christian saints and martyrs never experienced material prosperity. Their focus was on seeking God's reign (Matt. 6:33). We are grateful for God's blessings. But our prayers should always be to remain faithful to the God we know in Jesus Christ.

54. Must we always forgive other people?

When we pray the Lord's Prayer we are committing ourselves to forgiving other people. "Forgive us our debts, as we also have forgiven our debtors" (Matt. 6:12) links our prayer for forgiveness of our "debts" (sin) with our pardoning or releasing others for the wrongs they have done to us.

This linkage of our prayer for mercy and our providing mercy to others in the form of forgiveness tells us we will always need to be in the forgiving business. Why? Simply because we ourselves will always need to seek God's forgiveness for our own sinful actions. This joining of our need from God and the need of others from us is commanded by Jesus himself.

Later in the New Testament, forgiveness is seen as a way of life for Christians. It is in Jesus Christ that we have "redemption, the forgiveness of sins" (Col. 1:14; Eph. 1:7). From this forgiveness comes our response as forgiven people—to forgive others: "Be kind to one another, tenderhearted, forgiving one another, as God in Christ has forgiven you" (Eph. 4:32; Col. 3:13).

Forgiveness is not the natural pull for us; it is not our normal response to being wrong. Revenge or "getting even" is more likely for us. We're caught up short when, like Peter, we wonder how often we must forgive someone who sins against us. Like Peter we wonder, perhaps as many as seven times? We're startled when Jesus says, "Not seven times, but I tell you, seventy-seven times" (Matt. 18:22; variant: "seventy times seven"; cf. Luke 17:1–4). This means we are to forgive without counting the number of times we do so.

Others will wrong us. At points we will not be able to forget their sins against us; the wounds will be too deep and painful. But forgiveness can offer a chance to look at the past in a new way, to recognize the offense and the hurt but to decide that this will not be determinative to the relationship. It is to decide to hand over the past to God and to seek a relationship of positive care and mutuality for the future. The power to forgive in this sense comes from the Holy Spirit and the love of Christ.

55. How often do we need to repent?

When timers became available on ovens, a popular slogan was "Set it and forget it." Even if the preacher preached too long, the pot roast wouldn't be burned because the oven would shut off automatically!

We may wish we could set our Christian life and forget it. We may wish we could become Christians, join the church, and put things on automatic pilot so we would no longer have to worry about temptation or sin or forgiveness. But the Christian life is not that easy. We are tempted, we sin, we need forgiveness.

One part of Christian life where "Set it and forget it" does not work is with repentance. Repentance means turning from sin and toward a new life where that sin no longer reigns. The Heidelberg Catechism notes two parts to repentance: "the dying of the old self and the birth of the new" (*BC* 4.088).

How often do we need to repent? Daily. We sin daily, so we need to repent daily. As the Second Helvetic Confession puts it, because we acknowledge Christ as "head and foundation of the Church," we rest on him, and we "daily renew" ourselves "by repentance" (*BC* 5.135).

Three dimensions are important (see *BC* 5.094). First, repentance is a gift of God. God's Spirit leads us to desire to walk in new ways. We do not initiate this on our own (2 Tim. 2:25). Second, we lament our sins (Psalm 51). Sorrow and genuine grief for what we have done is part of the dying to self, which is repentance. Third, confession of sin to God expresses what we have done wrong—as the prodigal son did to his father (Luke 15:21) and the tax collector did in Jesus' parable (Luke 18:13).

Jesus promises that "anyone who comes to me I will never drive away" (John 6:37). When we confess our sin, our sin will be forgiven (1 John 1:9). This is our assurance.

Our daily repentance is not automatic or perfunctory. It arises from the genuineness of our sorrow for our sin, our confession, and our "strong desire to live according to the will of God in all good works" (*BC* 4.090).

56. What are the parts of prayer?

There are many kinds of prayer. Some are formal, perhaps written and used in corporate worship. Others are informal, spoken verbally or within us and expressed any time the Spirit moves us to pray. All prayers are heard by God, no matter what their form or when or how they are offered.

When prayers are formulated, it is helpful to recognize they can have different parts. Prayer functions in many ways. There are parts of prayer that convey different dimensions of our worship of God. Prayer is a form of worship. As there are parts of worship, so the parts of prayer give voice to ways we communicate with God in attitudes of worship.

The parts of prayer are often described as these:

Adoration. Psalms of praise (e.g., Ps. 100) pour forth the expressions of the heart that praise God for who God is and what God has done. We acknowledge God's greatness, love, and mercy. We give God all honor and glory and express our commitment as God's people.

Confession. In the midst of praise, we also recognize our sinfulness (Ps. 51) and need of God's forgiveness (Ps. 32). Sin affects our relationship with the God who loves us, and we seek a restoration of trust and love as well as God's mercy in pardoning us.

Thanksgiving is a part of prayer in which God's goodness is remembered and expressed (Ps. 107; 118). Gratitude is rendered for help and deliverance and for God's expressions of blessings. Thanksgiving is our response for God's ongoing care and protection.

Supplication is calling on God (Ps. 50:15) for all requests. These include prayers on behalf of others (intercession) and for ourselves. These are petitions for help (Ps. 28:2) and requests for God's action in situations and in the course of events.

Together, the first letters of these parts of prayer spell "acts." This reminds us that the natural extension of prayer and the means by which prayers are often answered is through human actions. In prayer, God's Spirit can prompt us and lead us to do something. This can enable God's will to be done and us to live as joyful children of God.

57. Why do we pray "in the name of Jesus Christ our Lord"?

Most of our formal prayers end with the phrase "in the name of Jesus Christ our Lord." Saying this has become perfunctory for us. It is almost like a code or like the phrase used in police radio calls years ago: "Over and out!"

But the phrase is important. It is used with good reason. It is a way of identifying our prayers with Jesus Christ, the one who, throughout the Gospels, encouraged his followers to pray (Matt. 6:5–14; Luke 11:5–12; John 14:13–14). Our prayer grows out of our faith in Jesus Christ. As it does, "in the name of Jesus Christ our Lord" reaches us in three ways.

This phrase is an *invitation* to pray. We may wonder why we should pray and if the great God of heaven hears our prayers. Is there a divine concern for us personally? As is sometimes asked, "Among so many, can God care; can special love be everywhere?" "In the name of Jesus Christ our Lord" reminds us we know God first and foremost through Jesus Christ. Jesus taught that God is approachable and knows us intimately. The one who knows us best, loves us most. God invites us to share the burdens and complexities of life in prayer, assuring us God hears and answers.

Second, this phrase is a *test* for our praying. It is not a magical formula to assure us we can get everything we want. Instead, it reminds us that our prayers should be ways of aligning ourselves with what God wants of us and of God's purposes for us. We listen, as well as speak, in prayer. Is what we are praying for or about something Jesus can bless?

Third, this phrase is the *power* in our prayer. Jesus Christ provides the power to help us live in the ways God wants us to live. Through him, no other power or situation or care is too much for him to overcome. When we pray "in the name of Jesus Christ our Lord," we are claiming the power of Jesus Christ as our own. We find in him all we need to meet whatever we face.

58. Must one have a "second baptism" in the Spirit to be a genuine Christian?

Churches in the Pentecostal tradition teach that when a person becomes a Christian and is baptized, that person also needs a "second baptism," in which one receives the baptism of the Holy Spirit.

The validity of this Spirit baptism is in the subsequent experience of speaking in tongues (Gr. *glossolalia*) and the practice of all the spiritual gifts mentioned in the New Testament. Without this baptism in the Spirit, one is not a genuine Christian.

Presbyterians do not believe in two baptisms. Baptism with water—for infants or adults—is a sign of our incorporation into the covenant family of God. There is "but one baptism in the Church of God; and it is sufficient to be once baptized or consecrated unto God. For baptism once received continues for all of life, and is a perpetual sealing of our adoption" (*BC* 5.186). Just as we do not seek a second baptism after being baptized as infants, so we do not seek a Spirit baptism different from our water baptism. For "baptism is a sacrament, wherein the washing with water, in the name of the Father, and of the Son, and of the Holy Ghost, doth signify and seal our ingrafting into Christ, and partaking of the benefits of the covenant of grace, and our engagement to be the Lord's" (*BC* 7.094).

This means for Presbyterians there is no two-step process for baptism as Christians. Baptism "marks the receiving of the same Spirit by all [Christ's] people. Baptism with water represents not only cleansing from sin, but a dying with Christ and a joyful rising with him to new life" (*BC* 9.51). The Holy Spirit gives "spiritual gifts" (Gr. *charisma*) to all Christians for the sake of the church (1 Cor. 12). So every Christian is a "charismatic." No one gift alone is ever the test of Christian faith. We do not await a second baptism to be sure our faith is genuine. Baptism is our assurance of our union with Christ in the covenant of grace, so "we might live a new life" (*BC* 5.187).

59. What is stewardship?

"Stewardship" is a common word in the church. It pops up especially during the fall, when churches begin to look toward their budgets for the next year. Hear the word "stewardship," and you reach for your wallet!

It's too bad such a rich term has been narrowed so much. The word "stewardship" (Gr. *oikonomia*) relates to the "steward" (Gr. *oikonomos*) who in biblical times was responsible for the planning and administration of a household (Gr. *oikos*). We are called to manage the resources God has given the human family throughout the earth (Gen. 1:26), as well as resources in the church (1 Cor. 4:1–2; Titus 1:7; 1 Pet. 4:10).

So "stewardship" is really a comprehensive term. Christian stewardship pervades the whole of life. Life itself comes from God and is to be lived for God's glory (1 Cor. 10:31). So in a true sense we can say, "Stewardship is my life!" It encompasses who we are and what we do. We gratefully receive what God has given and use all we have and all we are for God's purposes.

The finances with which the church is concerned is certainly part of this. Churches need these resources to carry out their missions and ministries. So our support for the stewardship program of the local church needs to be strong and deep. Where better to give our money than for the church's work, both where we are and throughout the world?

But there are other forms of stewardship as well. We are stewards of our time, our talents, our energies, our resources—no matter what they may be. Sometimes we hear we should "tithe" our money to the church, that is, give 10 percent of our incomes for the work of the church. This is a good goal for stewardship season and beyond. Yet not 10 percent but 100 percent of ourselves is our stewardship to God. God created us, redeemed us, and loved us in Jesus Christ. We give our whole lives to God, in all their dimensions, as "good stewards of the manifold grace of God" (1 Pet. 4:10).

60. Does God call us to specific work or specific jobs?

In the New Testament there is one "call" to all people. It is from Jesus Christ, who called his disciples: "Follow me" (Matt. 4:19; Mark 2:14). This is the call of the Christian gospel for persons to believe and follow Jesus Christ. This calling originates with God and is a call that summons the whole world.

"Calling" (or "vocation," from the Latin *vocatio*) in the Middle Ages changed from the basic call to faith in Jesus Christ into the call for a Christian to enter the monastic life or life as a nun or priest. One's calling or vocation was marked by this transition to a new religious life. "Vocation" meant only this unique calling to be a "religious," as the term is used in the Roman Catholic Church.

During the Protestant Reformation, the original New Testament use of "calling" was rediscovered. Martin Luther and John Calvin recognized that all Christians are "called." We are called not just to specifically religious service. We are called to serve God in the world in all we do.

This means different types of work or activities can be undertaken as ways of serving God and can be our calling. Primarily, our calling is who we are as Christians. Relatedly, God can call us to various ways of service, either as "jobs" or in places of service, such as the home. Through these we live out our vocation as Christians.

There's a story of a farmer's son who became a preacher. After several years of disappointment in his ministry, his father asked him why he had become a preacher. The son replied that he had had a dream in which he saw the letters "P.C." in the sky and knew this meant "Preach Christ." His mother said, "Perhaps P.C. really meant 'Plant corn'!" God may call us either to "preach Christ" in a formal way or to "plant corn." Each can be a calling we can follow as Presbyterian Christians.

The church is the people called by God to serve Jesus Christ. God grants good gifts to be used for the common good in the church and the world. Our vocation is who we are and what we do. Through it all, we "do everything for the glory of God" (1 Cor. 10:31).

61. What are the main ministries of the church?

When you look at the average Presbyterian church, you may think, "This church does a lot!" On a variety of fronts, in a typical week or month, the different types of events, meetings, and activities that go on in the church and among church members is significant. So we may wonder what it is that holds all this together.

There are a number of perspectives on the ministries of the church that can answer that question. One way to understand it all, however, is to recognize what the Presbyterian Church (U.S.A.) calls the "great ends of the church." These are six elements that have been part of the church for over a century. They are found in the opening chapter of the *Book of Order* and function as a kind of "mission statement" to describe the great purposes for which the church exists and does what it does.

- The proclamation of the gospel for the salvation of humankind
- The shelter, nurture, and spiritual fellowship of the children of God
- The maintenance of divine worship
- The preservation of the truth
- The promotion of social righteousness
- The exhibition of the Kingdom of Heaven to the world

These great aims give the church direction and offer a vision of Christian life together as the Presbyterian Church (U.S.A.) and, even more, as the church of Jesus Christ. They all relate to each other. The church proclaims the gospel in both word and deed. The church nurtures its members and engages in outward mission to the world. The church worships, and the church preserves the truth of the gospel of Christ.

These "great ends of the church" provide direction for churches. They also pose challenges. The church not only "is," but it "does." What it does reflects who it is, and who it is, is expressed in what it does. All our activities in the church—and in our individual lives as well—should be expressions of these "great ends." They help us realize who we are and whose we are. From these great ends the "ordinary" ministries of the church flow. Through these God is glorified and Jesus Christ is praised.

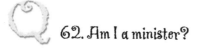

62. Am I a minister?

As Christians, we are all ministers of Jesus Christ. In the church, the body of Christ, we carry out the ministries Jesus began during his life. All of us are called to be ministers of Christ, no matter where we are or what we do.

For centuries, the church has had the "clergy"/"laity" split. It has set persons apart in ordination to carry out important and specific tasks of ministry, but we know all Christians are ministers. We are all called to follow Jesus Christ, continuing the ministries Jesus enacted during his days on earth.

In the Presbyterian Church, we do not formally ordain everyone the way we ordain ministers of Word and Sacrament or elders or deacons. But their ordination reminds us of our own calling to be ministers. We believe that in baptism and in our union with Christ, to be part of the church means we have ministries to live out on behalf of Jesus Christ and for his sake (*BC* 9.51).

The word "minister" comes from the Greek term *diakonia*, meaning "service." In the early church, "servants" or "deacons" were those who waited on tables, providing for those in need (Acts 6:1–6). But in the church we are all "deacons" or "servants," just as our Master said he had come "not to be served but to serve" (Mark 10:45). We serve, from Jesus' example, in word and deed (Luke 24:19). He proclaimed God's Word and "went about doing good" (Acts 10:38).

We are enabled to be ministers by God's Spirit, for "each member is the church in the world, endowed by the Spirit with some gift of ministry" (*BC* 9.38; 1 Cor. 12). The amazing variety of the Spirit's work is expressed in the amazing variety of people in the church and in their gifts for ministry. We do not all serve the same way. We do not all have very visible ministries of service. But all of us are ministers—clergy and laity alike. There are no gradations of ministries, no hierarchies. This would go against the direction of the one who washed his disciples' feet and said his disciples should do the same with each other (John 13:1–20).

63. Do Presbyterians believe in deathbed conversions?

Rabbi Eliezer once said, "Repent the day before you die." Since we do not know the day of our death, repentance should be an everyday practice!

Some people have never repented and have lived their whole lives outside the circle of any religious faith. Christianity recognizes this as an expression of our nature as sinners when no desire to live in relationship with God has been part of a person's experience.

Some persons come to a religious experience, in the case of Christianity to a faith in Jesus Christ as Lord and Savior, near their point of death. They can only express what is real to them then, having no chance to live life as a Christian.

These "deathbed conversions" are often viewed as suspect. There is no changed behavior or way of assessing whether someone's expression of faith at the point of death is genuine or not. Fortunately, it is not our place to make these judgments anyway. This belongs to God. God knows the heart, and God is the one with whom all of us have to deal, in this life and beyond.

One of the dying criminals on the cross asserted Jesus' innocence and asked Jesus to remember him "when you come into your kingdom." Jesus responded, "Truly I tell you, today you will be with me in Paradise" (Luke 23:39–43). This has traditionally been seen as indicating that it is possible for a person to receive the gift of salvation at the point of death, even when there is no opportunity to give expression to a Christian confession by participation in the sacraments or living and serving through a church community.

Presbyterians affirm God is free and can give grace for salvation in whatever ways God chooses and at whatever time God chooses. So a person can come to express faith in Jesus Christ as a gift of God's grace at the ending point of physical life. God's love can embrace a whole life of lived indifference or hostility to the gospel, for "gracious is the Lord, and righteous; our God is merciful" (Ps. 116:5).

5

Worship and Sacraments

64. How do Presbyterians observe Sunday?

The Jewish Sabbath was established as the seventh day of the week to remember God's rest from the work of creation (Gen. 2:3). It was the day for worship. Israel was commanded to "remember the Sabbath day, and keep it holy" (Exod. 20:8–10).

Early Christian worship, however, was on the first day of the week (Acts 20:7; 1 Cor. 16:2). This celebrated the day of the resurrection of Jesus Christ (Mark 16:2). The Westminster Confession notes that God has "particularly appointed one day in seven for a Sabbath, to be kept holy unto him: which, from the beginning of the world to the resurrection of Christ, was the last day of the week; and, from the resurrection of Christ, was changed into the first day of the week, which in Scripture is called the Lord's Day, and is to be continued to the end of the world as a Christian Sabbath" (*BC* 6.118). The Second Helvetic Confession understands things differently: "We do not believe that one day is any holier than another, or think that rest in itself is acceptable to God. Moreover, we celebrate the Lord's Day and not the Sabbath as a free observance" (*BC* 5.225).

The Westminster Confession urges a strict observance of the Lord's Day as a day of rest and worship, away from "works, words, and thoughts" about "worldly employments and recreations." The whole time is to be devoted to "public and private exercises of [God's] worship, and in the duties of necessity and mercy" (*BC* 6.119). In the United States, many "blue laws" relating to Sunday originated from this general prescription observed by American Puritans of the Reformed tradition.

Today, most Presbyterians do not practice a rigorous observance of Sunday, seeing that it can be a day to enjoy God's good gifts. Jesus healed (Matt. 12:1–14) and taught on the Sabbath (Mark 6:1–2). However, there is growing recognition of the need to step back from our normal activities and for the sake of our spirits and well-being observe a "sabbath" in which we consciously cultivate ways of renewal, rest, and worship. This spiritual discipline recognizes the importance of the biblical commandment, observed in ways the Christian finds as responsible means of faithful discipleship.

65. Why do we pray for others in worship services?

Prayers for others are prayers of intercession. Through them, we remember others before God and ask God to help others in various ways.

In prayer, we acknowledge God's presence and care for all life. We pray for others on a regular basis in worship out of Christian love and concern. For us as Presbyterians, all we believe about God as creator, sustainer, and redeemer is focused in our prayers for the ongoing life of the world, the church, and our fellow humans. The net of our care and concern is as wide as the heart of God and the compassion of Jesus Christ (Mark 6:34).

We recognize the need to pray in support of the whole people of God throughout the world in the church, those who are governing authorities in the world, and those who face difficulties and needs. Prayers of intercession focus our attention in worship on the world around us and the ongoing needs of others, which we realize are always present.

Our prayers of intercession also focus on the life and ministries of our local congregations and the pressing needs there. In the church's fellowship are needs of many kinds. We pray for those who need health and healing, who face personal problems, who are contemplating important decisions, who suffer grief and loss, and who have marriages and families facing difficulties, among others.

We are confident in our prayers of intercession, believing God hears and answers them. When we pray for others, prayer changes us, since by listening to God's Spirit we can be led to help others in important and meaningful ways. In prayer we speak and listen to God. We never know the ways by which the needs expressed in intercessory prayers in worship may be met by God in Christ, through the work of the Holy Spirit—even using us to be a means of "answering" those prayers for others.

Prayer matters. It can transform a congregation by engaging human needs with God's purposes. Prayer can transform us as we hear and act in ways that can bring life and hope.

66. What is the church year, and do Presbyterians follow it?

We check our calendars frequently, whether paper or electronic. They mark our time and give us a sense of the flow of our days.

The same is true in the church. The church year, marked by changing times and seasons, gives us opportunities to live in recognition that "my times are in your hand" (Ps. 31:15).

The ancient Jewish calendar revolved around God's liberation of the people from Egypt. Feasts and festivals were observed for worship of what God had done.

The Christian calendar centers on Jesus Christ. There are three major cycles. The first is the Christmas cycle. The church year begins with Advent, anticipating Jesus' birth. Christmas celebrates Christ's birth, and Epiphany marks Christ's manifestation to the Gentiles.

The second cycle is Ordinary Time, divided into two periods. The first period begins after Epiphany and continues to Ash Wednesday. The Baptism of the Lord is celebrated on the first Sunday of Ordinary Time, and the Transfiguration of the Lord is the last Sunday.

The third cycle is the Easter Cycle. Lent is the season of forty weekdays and six Sundays, beginning on Ash Wednesday. In Lent, the church anticipates the death of Christ. At the end of Lent, there are two periods: (1) the beginning of Holy Week, which starts with Passion/Palm Sunday; and (2) the Three Days, consisting of Maundy Thursday, Good Friday, and the Easter Vigil. Easter season is fifty days, including seven Sundays, beginning with Easter Day, when we celebrate the Resurrection of the Lord. Ascension Day is forty days after Easter. The Day of Pentecost, remembering the gift of the Holy Spirit to the church, ends the Easter cycle.

The rest of the church year is the second portion of Ordinary Time, as the church lives out its mission and ministry, empowered by the Spirit. Trinity Sunday begins this period, which extends until Christ the King (Reign of Christ) Sunday.

The church year gives us ways to mark the rhythms of our lives. Most Presbyterian churches observe nearly all the days and seasons, with variations in emphasis or celebrations. Other special days are recognized as well, depending on local customs and times of particular importance for a local Presbyterian church.

67. What are the parts of worship?

Presbyterian worship is often structured around several major parts. There are a number of worship rubrics that may be used as elements in these parts.

Gathering. God takes the initiative in calling us to worship. So a call to worship, hymn of praise, confession and pardon, and the passing of the peace of Christ are usual elements in the opening of worship.

The Word. For Presbyterians, reading, proclaiming, and hearing God's Word form a central core of worship. An anthem may be sung. A prayer for illumination by the Holy Spirit may precede readings from the Scriptures. The sermon is an exposition of God's Word in proclamation. Affirmations of faith, hymns, and responses to the Word follow. Baptism is administered in response to the Word. Prayers of the people may be offered. Tithes and offerings are received with prayer. The Lord's Supper (Eucharist) is also a response to the Word of God read and proclaimed.

Sending. Acts of commitment or discipleship are further expressions of response. Announcements for the church's life may be made and a hymn sung. A charge and blessing sends the congregation into the world by the power of the Holy Spirit.

Another pattern, marking the great moments of worship, comes from Isaiah's vision of God in the temple (Isa. 6:1–8).

Adoration of God. Isaiah is called into the presence of God (vv. 1–3).

Confession and forgiveness. Isaiah recognizes his sinfulness (vv. 4–5) and is cleansed (vv. 6–7).

God's word and response. Isaiah hears God's call to serve and responds, "Here am I; send me" (v. 8).

The emphasis in Presbyterianism is on the worship of the God who initiates the call to worship and draws the people of God together in the name of Jesus Christ, by the work of the Holy Spirit. Worship is focused on the triune God. It is not entertainment for the sake of the congregation! Worship is our response to the God who created us, loves us in Christ, and who draws the community of saints together by the Spirit. We praise God, pray to God, hear God's Word, and commit ourselves in obedience and service.

68. Why do we have hymns in worship?

Hymns (Gr. *hymnos*) are songs of praise rendered to God. We find hymns throughout the Old Testament. The Psalms are a collection of praises. The New Testament church sang "psalms and hymns and spiritual songs" to God (Eph. 5:19; Col. 3:16).

Hymns focus on the greatness and goodness of God, expressing in both text and tune the person and works of God. Christian hymns extol the triune God as Father, Son, and Holy Spirit. They proclaim God's greatness, sovereignty, majesty, love, mercy, and goodness—among other attributes. Praise finds its focus in God's "indescribable gift" in Jesus Christ (2 Cor. 9:15). This Christian impulse continues that of the psalmist: "I will give thanks to the Lord with my whole heart; I will tell of all your wonderful deeds. I will be glad and exult in you; I will sing praise to your name, O Most High" (Ps. 9:1–2; cf. 95:1–2).

Historically, Reformed churches have given the Psalms (the Psalter) an important place in their worship. There have been disagreements about whether it is proper to use anything other than psalms in worship since these are the words of Scripture. But Presbyterians in the United States decided it was also proper to use hymns in worship. Thus we have produced hymnals that provide an array of historic and contemporary hymns through which a congregation can praise God.

Hymns are a major part of Presbyterian worship because they enable us to express our deepest sense of praise and dependence on the God who has created, sustained, and loved us in Jesus Christ. Through hymns, we are able to express our faith through the words and music of others with whom we share Christian faith in the great "household of God" (Eph. 2:19). Hymns are a means of grace by which we can enter into the faith of the church and give voice to our own faith in ways we would not be capable of doing without the gifts of text and tune.

Hymns help us carry out the psalmist's wish: "Let the peoples praise you, O God; let all the peoples praise you" (Ps. 67:5).

69. What is the declaration/assurance of pardon in the worship service?

Presbyterians have a declaration or assurance of pardon in our worship services because we need it! We need it every time we worship.

A confession of sin is part of our worship services because we need that also. God calls us to worship; in response, we recognize who we are in relation to God. We are sinners. We cannot get rid of sin by ourselves, so we confess our sin.

Then we need to hear a word of forgiveness! Sometimes called a "declaration" or "assurance" of pardon, or a "declaration of forgiveness," this is a statement that God hears our prayers of confession and gives us wonderful, cleansing forgiveness of our sins in Jesus Christ. God's forgiving grace is sure, based on the promises of Scripture (1 John 1:9). God's forgiveness comes through Jesus Christ (1 Tim. 1:15; 1 Pet. 2:24), who died for us (Rom. 8:34) and brings us new life (2 Cor. 5:17).

Some ask how the worship leader can "announce" forgiveness, since we cannot know if a confession of sin by worshipers is genuine or not, since we must truly be sorry for our sins. The good news is that it is not up to us to validate this declaration of forgiveness or to administer this assurance of pardon. That is up to God! Presbyterians believe it is by the Holy Spirit that we are led to confess our sins and that the Spirit is the one who knows whether we are genuinely sorry for our sins or are just "mouthing the words."

Likewise, the Holy Spirit makes the declaration of forgiveness and the assurance of pardon effective in our lives. We don't do that ourselves, and no one else can know the intentions of our hearts. So it is entirely appropriate to announce forgiveness through Jesus Christ, based on the Scriptures' promises. The Spirit seals God's forgiveness within us. We are confident God's Spirit has led us to confess, and through the Spirit the love and mercy of God in Jesus Christ becomes real so we can experience forgiveness of sins.

70. Why is there an offering collected in each worship service?

𝓐n offering (sometimes colloquially called the "collection") is part of our worship service for both practical and theological reasons. The practical reason is the church needs the financial support of the congregation to carry out its mission and ministries. The offering is a means by which people can support the work of the church in an ongoing way. Many church members pledge to the church, promising to provide amounts of money each week, month, or year. The offering is a way this support can be carried out and the pledges fulfilled.

But the theological reasons for an offering in each worship service relate to what giving our finances points to in our Christian lives. Our whole lives as Christians are an "offering" or a "living sacrifice" to God (Rom. 12:1). For Jesus Christ offered up himself on our behalf (Eph. 5:2; Heb. 10:10). Our offering is of ourselves, in all dimensions of who we are and what we do. We give ourselves to God in Christ, open to God's Spirit to guide, direct, and work within us that which is "pleasing to the Lord" (Eph. 5:10; cf. Col. 1:10; 1 John 3:22).

Theologically, our response in offering our monetary resources is as a symbol of the offering of ourselves. We respond in thankfulness for God's grace in giving Jesus Christ to the world and electing and calling us to be the people of God. We have gratitude in our hearts (Col. 3:16) and are thankful (Col. 3:15). A clear way to express our gratefulness is through support of the church's work in the world, both locally and beyond.

In contemporary life, people support the church financially by writing checks, using credit cards, or having their bank accounts debited. In a sense, it is too bad when they take the "automatic" route that they simply pass the offering plate. But passing the plate can still be an act of worship. When we receive the plate, we recall the meaning of the offering. We dedicate ourselves anew to God's purpose, praying with the psalmist: "Accept my offerings of praise, O Lord, and teach me your ordinances" (Ps. 119:108).

71. What is the lectionary?

Presbyterians often see "lectionary" used in bulletins or church newsletters. Usually there will be Bible passages listed as the "lectionary readings" for a particular Sunday. This is much more common today than it was forty or fifty years ago.

A lectionary (Lat. *legere*, "to read") is a set of readings from Scripture that have been established for use in worship services of the church. The Revised Common Lectionary (RCL) is a whole set of readings for each Sunday and festival of the church. It has been prepared by the Consultation on Common Texts and is used by many major Christian churches in North America.

The lectionary texts are set in three-year cycles: Years A, B, and C. Each lectionary occasion features a reading from the Old Testament, Psalms, Gospels, and Epistles. Portions of these groups are prescribed in sequence for many of the occasions of Ordinary Time, when there are no special seasons or festivals of the church year. Appropriate readings for the seasons of Christmas, Lent, and Easter, along with other festivals, are featured.

The purpose of the lectionary is so a whole range of Scripture will be heard throughout the years in the church's worship. "Lectionary preachers" still choose on what passage(s) of Scripture to consider in sermons. Sometimes several or all the passages are brought into the sermon; other times, a sermon may focus on just one passage.

Since the Roman Catholic Church's Vatican II council (1962–1965), there has been a renewed interest in liturgy, and consequently in the lectionary, among Roman Catholics and Protestants. Among the benefits of lectionary use is that these common Bible readings used in churches across denominations on any one Sunday remind us of the unity of the church. Preachers often note that using the lectionary keeps them from preaching on just their "favorite" passages, since they discipline themselves to preach on the prescribed biblical passages.

Many Presbyterian pastors use the lectionary texts in worship for preaching. But using the lectionary is not required in Presbyterian churches. Adaptations are often made in local situations for special events or for a period of time.

A daily lectionary is also available. It enables one to read through the New Testament twice and the Old Testament once in a two-year cycle.

72. How does preaching become effective?

Week after week, year after year, preachers preach and congregations listen. What happens?

Presbyterians have always emphasized preaching. Our Reformed tradition, going back to John Calvin, has seen preaching as central for the church. The Scots Confession, echoing Calvin, says that the "notes of the true Kirk [church]" are "first, the true preaching of the Word of God" (*BC* 3.18).

Preaching is crucial for the church since "faith comes from what is heard, and what is heard comes through the word of Christ" (Rom. 10:17). Preaching is the means by which the gift of faith in Jesus Christ is given by the Holy Spirit. To the question of where faith originates, the Heidelberg Catechism says, "The Holy Spirit creates it in our hearts by the preaching of the holy gospel, and confirms it by the use of the holy Sacraments" (*BC* 4.065; 7.089; 7.265).

Perhaps astonishingly, the Second Helvetic Confession affirms that "the preaching of the Word of God is the Word of God" (*BC* 5.004). Preaching should be based on Scripture and its interpretation. Through preaching "the very Word of God is proclaimed, and received by the faithful" (*BC* 5.004). But how does preaching become effective? What happens in preaching?

From one point of view, nothing happens through preaching. Congregations listen politely, but what outward effects are perceived?

Our confessions answer that we do not believe "outward preaching is to be thought as fruitless because the instruction in true religion depends on the inward illumination of the Spirit" (*BC* 5.005). Preaching becomes effective through the Holy Spirit. When and where and how the Spirit will choose to use the preaching of the Word is not within our—or the preacher's—prerogative to know. We cannot say what happens in preaching in any situation. We can believe the power of God's Spirit can make preaching effect a difference in a life, at any time and in any place. The excitement of preaching—for preacher and congregation—is in the unexpected, even seemingly nonapparent effects the Spirit may enable. So we preach and we listen—expectantly!

73. What are the different modes of baptism?

Presbyterians are used to seeing baptism administered through the sprinkling of water on a person's head, either an infant's or an adult's. But not all Christian denominations administer baptism this way.

There are three "modes" of baptism. *Immersion* is when a person is fully submerged under water. Some denominations, especially Baptist traditions, insist this is the only valid mode of baptism (Gr. *baptizein*, "to dip in water"). The baptism of Jesus was the model for baptism in the early church, and Jesus was baptized by John the Baptist in the Jordan River (Mark 1:9). In *pouring* (Lat. *affusio*, "to pour on"), water is poured over the head of the person being baptized. Churches that practice pouring often baptize infants as well as adults. They recognize other modes of baptism as legitimate. *Sprinkling* (Lat. *aspergere/aspersio*, "to sprinkle") is used by churches that recognize both infant and adult baptism. It involves the sprinkling of a small amount of water on the head of the one being baptized. All three modes can appeal to New Testament accounts and early church tradition as precedents.

Reformed Christians have not considered the mode of baptism as significant. The Westminster Confession says, "Dipping of the person into the water is not necessary, but baptism is rightly administered by pouring or sprinkling water upon the person" (*BC* 6.156).

Most important are the theological meanings of baptism. Baptism is with water, which "washes dirt away, and cools and refreshes hot and tired bodies. And the grace of God performs these things for souls, and does so invisibly or spiritually" (*BC* 5.188).

What is key—regardless of the mode—is to realize "there is

but one baptism in the Church of God; and it is sufficient to be once baptized or consecrated unto God. For baptism once received continues for all of life, and is a perpetual sealing of our adoption" (*BC* 5.186). Baptism has ongoing effects. It confers our identities as children of God and shapes our lives in God's service in Jesus Christ by the work of the Holy Spirit.

74. What is believer's baptism?

Believer's baptism is a feature of Anabaptism, a Protestant tradition that originated in the sixteenth century but that rejected the theologies of Luther and Calvin. Its name comes from its insistence on rebaptism (from Gr. *ana*, "again," and *baptein*, "to dip in water") for those baptized as infants, which was the practice of the followers of Luther and Calvin, as well as of the Roman Catholic Church. Anabaptists believe the only valid baptism is one administered to adults who are able to confess their faith in Jesus Christ.

Both Luther and Calvin rejected this view of baptism. They believed baptism is a sign of God's grace. Its efficacy does not rest on the person making the profession of faith, but on God's grace given in Christ, of which the sacrament of baptism is a sign and seal. The emphasis in baptism is on God's initiative in electing us into the covenant of grace in Christ, not on presenting one's own faith as the reason for baptism. The danger is to see one's own profession as giving one the right to merit being baptized. This would make baptism dependent on oneself and turn one's profession of faith into a "work" deserving something from God.

Presbyterians believe that

> [infants] as well as their parents, are included in the covenant and belong to the people of God. Since both redemption from sin through the blood of Christ and the gift of faith from the Holy Spirit are promised to these children no less than to their parents, infants are also by baptism, as a sign of the covenant, to be incorporated into the Christian church and distinguished from the children of unbelievers. This was done in the Old

Covenant by circumcision. In the New Covenant baptism has been instituted to take its place. (*BC* 4.074)

Baptism is receiving the gift of belonging to Jesus Christ, by God's grace. Receiving baptism as a helpless infant reminds us of the nature of salvation itself as being by God's free grace to sinners (Rom. 5:6–8; Eph. 2:8–9). When we say "baptism," we say "grace"—for sinners who now receive "newness of life" (Rom. 6:3–4).

 ## 75. How often should the Lord's Supper be celebrated?

This is a question every Presbyterian congregation faces. Changing the Communion schedule can sometimes present challenges, since it means a change in the rhythm of a church's life and practices.

In sixteenth-century Geneva, John Calvin wanted to have the Lord's Supper celebrated in each service of Sunday worship, since he believed both the preaching of the Word and the sacraments were means of God's revelation to us. However, the city officials thought this would make the sacrament seem too commonplace, so they restricted the number of observances. Calvin arranged for different Geneva churches to celebrate the Supper on different Sundays, so one could "itinerate" to a Supper observance each week.

The Reformed leader Huldrych Zwingli (1484–1531) advocated observing the Supper four times per year—once in the autumn and on Christmas, Easter, and Pentecost. In Scotland, four times per year was a norm from 1562, but it later became only annually. The Scottish and Zwinglian practices influenced the U.S. Presbyterians, who usually observed the Lord's Supper once a quarter.

Particularly after the 1960s, during the period of heightened liturgical interest, it became customary for Presbyterian churches to celebrate the sacrament more frequently. The tenor of the service also changed, from the traditional somberness with its emphasis on sin and repentance to a mode of celebration as found in the Lord's Supper liturgy in *The Worshipbook* (1970): "Friends: This is the joyful feast of the people of God."

Now it is common to have monthly celebrations of the Lord's Supper, and in churches with multiple worship services, one service each week may include the Supper. The Supper is also celebrated on other special occasions in the life of the church, and especially on Maundy Thursday.

It is appropriate for all Presbyterian worship services to include the Lord's Supper, since Word and sacrament go together and are marks of the church (*BC* 3.18). The Lord's Supper is always preceded by the reading and proclamation of the Word. The frequency of the Lord's Supper is set by the session. It should be celebrated frequently enough (not less than quarterly) for congregations to recognize its importance and vitality for worship and Christian life.

76. In what ways can I worship in my personal life?

Our identity as Christians flows from our union with Jesus Christ (Gal. 2:19–20) and our life in the worshiping community of the church. It is important to realize that as Christians we are communal creatures. We are elected and called into the body of Christ through baptism and faith, with our Christian lives lived in the context of the church community.

We worship communally but also in personal acts of worship and Christian commitment as disciples of Jesus Christ. Worship shapes our identities and enables us to see the world through the "theological eyeglasses" of the purposes and grace of God. Our lives move in the rhythms of worship and discipleship, discipleship and worship.

In addition to corporate worship, we carry out ways of personal worship so we may do all things for the glory of God (1 Cor. 10:31) and "take every thought captive to obey Christ" (2 Cor. 10:5). Among these elements of personal worship are the following:

Bible reading. Meditation on Scripture grows out of a love of

Scripture, expressed by the psalmist, who said, "I treasure your word in my heart" (Ps. 119:11). Scripture can be read in many ways. A "devotional" reading will ask, "What is God saying to me in this passage of Scripture?"

Prayer. Prayer is conversation with God. The goal of "pray without ceasing" (1 Thess. 5:17; cf. Rom. 12:12) points both to set times of prayer as well as spontaneous prayers. The goal is a constant sense of the presence of God in life.

Families and households. Times of Bible reading, prayer, singing, and giving and sharing are ways personal worship in the contexts of daily life can be expressed.

Vocation. Our call and our opportunities to serve God in a variety of ways in our daily lives, occupations, and relationships with others are ways we recognize God's presence. We express our faith through our vocational identity as acts of personal worship.

Service in church and world. Our service to church and in the world in varieties of ways can be seen as expressions of worship. We do it all, since "the love of Christ urges us on" (2 Cor. 5:14).

77. What is the purpose of a funeral service?

A funeral service bears witness to the resurrection of Jesus Christ as central to our Christian faith. This is in the midst of the sadness, grief, and loss experienced by those who love the one who has died.

Presbyterian practice is to prefer the service be seen as a "Witness to the Resurrection," take place in the church, under the direction of the pastor, and with the church community gathered, along with friends and family of the deceased. The funeral service is a worship service with the usual elements of worship being observed, including prayers, readings from Scripture, a sermon, and hymns. There may be a place in the service where aspects of the life of the one who died are mentioned. But the primary focus of the service is not to eulogize the deceased but to witness to the hope of the gospel with the Christian community, even in the midst of tears. The service commends the one who has died to God's eternal care, and the people receive a benediction commending them to God's care. A gravesite committal service also commends the deceased to God's care and witnesses to the resurrection hope of eternal life.

The Presbyterian emphasis on the centrality of the resurrection of Jesus Christ means a worship service at the time of death can convey elements of joy and hope in the midst of the sorrow and grief of those who gather. Jesus wept at the death of his friend Lazarus (John 11:35), but he also promised, "I am the resurrection and the life. Those who believe in me, even though they die, will live, and everyone who lives and believes in me will never die" (John 11:25–26). We recognize the human emotional realities associated with physical death. But our vision is also lifted beyond ourselves in sadness to the promise of resurrected life in the presence of the triune God.

For those remaining, Jesus' promise "Blessed are those who mourn, for they will be comforted" (Matt. 5:4) is real. The community of faith can be important in enabling those who face loss to find hope in real and tangible ways and to help sustain faith in difficult days.

6

Social-Ethical Issues

78. What sources inform our ethical decisions?

Presbyterian Christians turn first to the Bible as a source to inform our ethical decisions. We believe Scripture is the Word of God, so the Bible is the primary place in which God's will is revealed and life guidance given to us. In the Reformed tradition, the law of God is seen to be primarily intended to instruct us as the people of God on how God wants us to live. Also, the person of Jesus is the norm for what it means to be truly human, and thus Jesus is the model by which our actions should be measured.

Appealing to the Bible, however, does not answer all our questions. When looking for ethical guidance in Scripture, we must be sensitive to biblical contexts and cultures. We should not simply transfer some biblical prescriptions into guidance for today. Biblical mentions of slavery, for example, do not mean slavery is a practice we should emulate today. We need to use the best resources possible to understand biblical texts if we turn to them for help in informing us on ethical issues.

The Bible has a unique and authoritative role for us. But other dimensions for helping us make ethical decisions are also important. Nonbiblical elements such as data from the natural and social sciences as well as human experience can inform our perceptions. As our own selves or characters are shaped and even transformed by considering many facets of an issue, we may see and hear biblical texts in new ways. Nonbiblical sources can be ways for the Christian community to experience God in the wider world. The church community itself can be a resource in helping us make personal ethical decisions. In a wider scope, the church can bring its own unique resources into dialogue with other sources of insight. Ethical decisions are often highly complex. We will not always make the right decisions. As we try to understand who God is calling us to be and what God wants us to do, we live by faith. We seek God's mercy and forgiveness when we fail or follow a wrong path.

79. Do Presbyterians believe in birth control?

Presbyterians and others in the Reformed tradition have not considered the primary purpose of marriage to be procreation. Marriage has many dimensions, and creation of offspring is an important one. But one significant decision for married couples is the number of children they wish to have. This is a decision to be made responsibly, under God.

The Presbyterian Church (U.S.A.) and its predecessor denominations have recognized this responsibility placed on couples in the procreative function. Today the church also sees that limits on population growth in a whole society can be understood as a way of caring for one's family now and for generations to come. Birth control is a primary and morally appropriate way by which family planning can take place.

The church has understood the gospel to mean all children born into the world are loved by God and should be provided with opportunities to have their needs met in equitable and just ways. Every child born into the world is of inestimable worth to God. The human family has responsibilities to use the world's environment so that humanity can flourish in ways that, from a Christian perspective, are in accord with the will of God. Fewer births leading to population stabilization have been recognized as a way to enhance this overall perspective.

The PC(USA) advocates access to contraceptives for both women and men. It has never advocated abortion as a form of birth control. It also respects and appreciates persons who, as an act of conscience, do not choose to conceive children. This decision should not be seen as irresponsible or contrary to Christian understandings of a faithful life.

The church has urged the study of sexuality at all levels to enable people to make good ethical decisions about procreation and their responsibilities as human and thus sexual beings, created by God. In marriage, couples are responsible for considering their callings as Christ's followers and deciding how they can live as faithful Christians with regard to matters of procreation.

8⊙. Why do Presbyterians believe the church should be active in society?

The church is active in society because the church lives in society. This seems obvious. But its implications are far-reaching.

The Reformed tradition has taken seriously the church as the *people of God*. God works in this world through the people God has chosen to serve God. Israel in the Old Testament was to be a "light to the nations" (Isa. 42:6) so that God's "salvation may reach to the end of the earth" (Isa. 49:6). The character of God is to be reflected in the corporate and personal lives of the people of God. This means God's concerns for justice, righteousness, peace, and mercy (Ps. 33:5; 85:8)—as proclaimed by the prophets (Amos 5:24; Micah 6:8)—are to be embodied in the life of the nation and in the relationships of people with each other.

The church as the people of God (Heb. 4:9) is to carry out God's work in the world, with concerns for the world itself and all its people. The Confession of 1967 says the church is "entrusted with God's message of reconciliation and shares God's labor of healing the enmities which separate people from God and from each other" (*BC* 9.31, inclusive language text; see http://pcusa.org/media/uploads/theologyandworship/pdfs/confess67.pdf for this text).

As the *body of Christ* (1 Cor. 12:27), the church continues the ministry of Jesus, who came "to seek out and to save the lost" (Luke 19:10). This means a concern for the whole person, "body" and "soul." The Reformed tradition has emphasized the work of deacons in the church. Their ministries of care are for all in need. They lead the congregation and the whole church in social ministries.

In the *freedom of the Spirit* (2 Cor. 3:17), the church engages the world by proclaiming the gospel of Christ in word and deed. Concerns for the structures of society, infected as they are by human sin, lead to proclaiming the gospel and taking actions to provide for the well-being of those God loves.

The church seeks to do the will of God, obey God, and minister in the midst of the world. Presbyterian churches can do nothing less than be fully active in society through countless ministries.

81. What should the attitude of Presbyterians be toward government?

Church-state relations have long been a contested issue. In the Protestant Reformation, the Lutheran, Reformed, and Anabaptist traditions developed differing views. The Anabaptist view was the most radical: the Christian should not participate in the "state" and should never serve as a "magistrate," since the Christian's "citizenship is in heaven" (Phil. 3:20).

The Reformed tradition has seen the "state" as a good gift of God. Those who exercise power in the state are to do so for God's glory "and the public good" (*BC* 6.127). Christians can participate in the state in leadership roles and ought to "maintain piety, justice, and peace, according to the wholesome laws of each commonwealth," in the language of the Westminster Confession (*BC* 6.128; cf. 5.252).

The basic New Testament prescription is this: "Let every person be subject to the governing authorities; for there is no authority except from God, and those authorities that exist have been instituted by God" (Rom. 13:1). Even in the Roman Empire, early Christians were told, "Fear God. Honor the emperor" (1 Pet. 2:17).

Reformed Christians have recognized the citizen's responsibility to obey the government and participate in government. The government is to provide for the public good and for the context where peace and justice are carried out.

In the early Reformed tradition, magistrates were seen as God's representatives, with responsibilities both for "tables of the law"—religion and worship—as well as for maintaining safety and peace. Today in the United States, with the separation of church and state, we do not look for elected officials to be God's "deputies" or "vicars." But we do expect leadership toward a society where governmental functions are carried out and civil responsibilities for safety, justice, and peace are administered equitably.

Presbyterian Christians will pray for government leaders (1 Tim. 2:1–2), pay taxes (Rom. 13:6–7), and be obedient to the law (Rom. 13:5; Titus 3:1). Yet, ultimately, God alone is Lord of the conscience, and our primary allegiance is always to God, above all human authorities (Acts 5:29). Many Presbyterians have participated in all levels of government as a calling through which they seek the glory of God and the common good for all.

82. Do people have the right to rebel against unjust governments?

During the American Revolution, some in England called the war a "Presbyterian rebellion." The term "Presbyterian" was used fairly loosely to describe Calvinists and those with anti-monarchical leanings. But it was true at its core. The new land had a strong Reformed ethos, and many Presbyterians fought on the side of the American patriots. A Presbyterian clergyman, John Witherspoon (1723–1794) signed the Declaration of Independence.

We pick and choose our revolutions, according to whether or not they seem "justified." The basic Reformed attitude to government is the recognition that governing authorities are "instituted by God" (Rom. 13:1). But what shall we do when Romans 13 turns to Revelation 13, or the struggles are between the powers of God and the powers of evil ("beasts"), those "rulers" and "powers" whose purpose and actions are counter to God's (Rom. 8:28; Col. 1:16)?

Reformed Christians have resisted governments when governments have acted in ways they believe are against God's will. The right of resistance has been a debated topic. Reformed Christians resisted the king violently in seventeenth-century England, during the English Revolution when the Westminster Confession of Faith (1647) was being written.

In the face of Nazi ideology, the Barmen Declaration (1934) proclaimed that "Jesus Christ, as he is attested for us in Holy Scripture, is the one Word of God which we have to hear and which we have to trust and obey in life and in death" (*BC* 8.10). It rejected as "false doctrine" that the state "should and could become the single and totalitarian order of human life" (*BC* 8.23). The Confessing Church in Germany sought to be true to the gospel in the midst of political oppression and injustice.

Deep tensions have existed in our tradition regarding the relation of church and state and whether there is a right to revolution— and what kind of revolution (violent/nonviolent?)—when the government in power acts contrary to God's ways. These have been expressed differently at various periods. But our basic stance is that of the apostles: "We must obey God rather than any human authority" (Acts 5:29; cf. 1 Cor. 7:23).

83. Can Christians participate in war?

Christians have participated in many wars throughout history. They have caused wars and have died in wars. Yet Christians have often agonized about this participation. The plain prohibition of the Ten Commandments, "You shall not murder" (Exod. 20:13), and the teachings of Jesus in reinforcing the commandment (Matt. 5:21; 19:18) show the direction of the divine intention is toward the preservation and nurturing of life, not death—and not massive deaths in war. Whatever one makes of Old Testament stories, when God's will was interpreted as to wage war, or of New Testament images of warfare, the vision of a world at peace (Isa. 2:4; Micah 4:3) and the simple prescription to "love your enemies" (Matt. 5:44) have been central to the Christian vision.

St. Augustine (354–430) articulated a "just war" theory from a Christian perspective that holds there are times when certain conditions are met that justify war theologically and ethically. This theory has been used often to legitimate warfare and the "rightness" of a nation's cause against enemies. It addresses when a nation may use armed force and what is acceptable in the use of that armed force. While the contexts of Augustine's day and our own are much different, the just war theory—and its elaborations by Thomas Aquinas (1225–1274) and others—is still prominent as a way of understanding when and why a nation may rightly engage in war.

Reformed Christians have held different views about the legitimacy of participating in war. Many have followed the just war theory, as seen by American Presbyterians' participation in wars carried out by the United States from the American Revolution to the present. Other Presbyterians, however, have urged pacifism, arguing armed force cannot be justified. In addition, given the present danger of escalating hostilities among nations with nuclear weapons and the potential obliteration of the planet, some argue for a "nuclear pacifism," claiming armed force is now too dangerous a strategy in which to engage.

Presbyterians seek to emphasize peacemaking as a primary understanding of the Christian gospel. We are "emissaries of peace" (*BC* 9.25) and of the God who reconciles "all things" (Col. 1:20) and who in Jesus Christ "is our peace" (Eph. 2:14). We recognize these prescriptions for peace while in specific situations we may disagree on appropriate action about war.

84. Where do we see the reign of God in the world?

We usually think of the reign or kingdom of God as in the future. We believe in heaven, eternal life, and the breathtaking pictures where angels sing,

"The kingdom of the world has become the kingdom of our Lord
and of his Messiah,
and he will reign forever and ever."

(Rev. 11:15)

Magnificent!
Yet the reign of God, while future, is also present. We pray in
the Lord's Prayer, "Your kingdom come. Your will be done, on
earth as it is in heaven" (Matt. 6:10; Luke 11:2). God's reign is
in process, taking shape here and now on earth. God's Spirit is at
work, God's power is operating, and the kingdom Jesus and his
disciples proclaimed has "come near" (Matt. 10:7).

The "kingdom parables" of Jesus tell us to be alert for signs of
God's reign. Can we see the work of God in the people, places,
and events of our lives? We will miss this if we look forward to
the kingdom as a "big bang," as something still to come. Instead,
we should be attentive to the little things of life, which gladdened
Jesus' heart because they pointed to what God is doing in the world
and ways God's will and reign are taking shape.

When God's word is shared (Matt. 13:1–8), when the sick
are healed (Luke 10:9), joy experienced (Matt. 13:44), when the
hungry are fed, the naked are clothed, and those in prison are visited
(Matt. 25:34–40), when the lost are found (Luke 15:8–10)—here
is the reign of God, right before our eyes!

Those things dear to the heart of Jesus and that he shared in his
preaching and teaching are what God values. They are signs of
God's reign right here, right now.

We anticipate the coming kingdom, which humans will not win
but which God will give. But "on our way to the kingdom," we see
glimpses of it, a "ferment in the world" (*BC* 9.54), anticipations to
bless our faith, encouraging us to plant the seeds of God's reign as
we love others, strive for justice, and proclaim God's peace.

7

The Future

85. What is Christian hope?

We like to be optimistic. We like to think things will work out, both for ourselves and for the world. We often say we hope for the best. Hope is part of the human spirit.

But Christian hope is different. Christian hope does not rest on ourselves or human possibilities. Christian hope is grounded in God, in God's action in Jesus Christ, and in the ongoing work of the Holy Spirit. The realities of Christian hope transcend all human optimism or "positive" thinking. The emphasis is on what God has done, is doing, and will do.

In God and God's word we hope (Ps. 43:5; 130:5). In hope we are saved through Jesus Christ (Rom. 8:24). We rejoice in hope (Rom. 12:12) as we have the hope of "sharing the glory of God" (Rom. 5:2).

Christian hope pervades our lives. As Presbyterians, we see God's work within us and among us, God's providence guiding our lives. We are energized by the hope that pulls us forward. The future is secure in what God has done in the death and resurrection of Jesus Christ. The end of history is certain: evil and sin are ultimately defeated. Jesus Christ "will reign forever and ever" (Rev. 11:15).

All our efforts now, in the church on behalf of all people, have meaning and significance because they are part of God's work in history for God's will. God's purposes will prevail. Our efforts are made possible by Jesus Christ, who is our hope (1 Tim. 1:1). Through his resurrection we are assured our labor is "not in vain"

(1 Cor. 15:58). No matter how tough life gets, this word of hope encourages us and enables us to trust God's future.

Jesus Christ is the ground and goal of hope (1 Pet. 1:21). He is the certainty of our hope, and in him we have the "hope of eternal life" God has promised (Titus 1:2). Human optimism can have its place. But most important is the hope linked with faith and love (1 Cor. 13:13). This comes from the one who has "given us a new birth into a living hope through the resurrection of Jesus Christ from the dead" (1 Pet. 1:3).

86. What about the Last Judgment?

The common picture of the Last Judgment is from Jesus' parable of the Sheep and the Goats (Matt. 25:31–46). In this parable, the "goats" will "go away into eternal punishment, but the righteous [i.e., sheep] into eternal life" (Matt. 25:46). This image is captured in the Westminster Confession: "God hath appointed a day, wherein he will judge the world in righteousness by Jesus Christ, to whom all power and judgment is given of the Father." Then "all persons, that have lived upon earth, shall appear before the tribunal of Christ, to give an account of their thoughts, words, and deeds; and to receive according to what they have done in the body, whether good or evil" (*BC* 6.180). It is then, too, that the elect receive eternal salvation and the "wicked" are punished with "everlasting destruction from the presence of the Lord" (*BC* 6.181).

We believe in the reality of judgment, as stated simply in the Apostles' Creed. Jesus Christ will "come to judge the quick [i.e., the living] and the dead" (*BC* 2.2). It is Jesus Christ who judges.

But the perspective of the Heidelberg Catechism and other Reformed confessions is helpful. The catechism speaks of the "comfort" of Christ's return to judge. This is to recognize that our Judge is also our Savior, Jesus Christ. Our comfort is that we await "the very Judge from heaven who has already submitted himself to the judgment of God for me" and that "he shall take me, together with all his elect, to himself into heavenly joy and glory" (*BC* 4.052). As the Confession of 1967 says, "All who put their trust in Christ face divine judgment without fear, for the judge is their redeemer" (*BC* 9.11).

Our gospel message is to proclaim to the world God loves (John 3:16) that "while we were enemies, we were reconciled to God through the death of his Son" (Rom. 5:10). Judgment is real (2 Tim. 4:1). But God has taken on our judgment in Jesus Christ (*BC* 9.14), and "mercy triumphs over judgment" (Jas. 2:13). We can face all "judgments" in life and ultimately the "last judgment" with confidence (1 John 2:28) and hope (Titus 2:13; 1 John 3:3).

87. Will evil be defeated in the end?

Yes. There will come a day when the evil powers that oppose God will be overcome by the invincible "Lord God Almighty" (Rev. 11:17) who reigns over all things.

We do not live in that day yet. For now, evil is real—all kinds of evil: rulers (Rom. 8:38; Titus 3:1), authorities (Eph. 3:10), cosmic powers (Eph. 6:12), and dominions (Col. 1:16) are rampant. Scripture indicates the present world is subject to "the evil one" (1 John 5:19; cf. Matt. 4:8–9; Rev. 17:18). This evil one, sometimes called "Satan" or "the devil" (Luke 4:6), is called the ruler of this world (John 12:31; 14:30; 2 Cor. 4:4; Eph. 2:2). Whether or not one believes in a personal devil, this evil is real. No wonder Jesus instructs us to pray, "Rescue us from the evil one" (Matt. 6:13).

But in the midst of this world, we are sustained by the victory Jesus Christ has already won over evil powers. On his way to the cross, Jesus proclaimed, "I watched Satan fall from heaven like a flash of lightning" (Luke 10:18). Through the cross, the "ruler of this world will be driven out" (John 12:31; Rev. 12:7-9). In his resurrection, Jesus Christ puts all "enemies under his feet" (1 Cor. 15:25), triumphs over enemies (Col. 2:15), and is the "head over all things" (Eph. 1:22). The victory has been won by Jesus Christ (1 Cor. 15:57).

For now, evil is down but not out. Ultimately the reign of evil is ended through the victory of Jesus Christ. But until that time when the reign of Christ is finally established, we deal with the powers of evil in our world and in our lives. We have our own temptations from the evil one (1 Pet. 5:8). Oppression, injustice, and violence persist. These are all attempts to turn us away from following Christ.

But in the cross and resurrection of Jesus Christ, we look to the ultimate consummation when evil is defeated, Satan is doomed (Rev. 20), and the "new heaven and new earth" (Rev. 21:1) become realities. Then "every tongue [will] confess that Jesus Christ is Lord to the glory of God the Father" (Phil. 2:11).

88. Do Presbyterians believe in purgatory?

In Roman Catholic theology, purgatory (Lat. *purgatorium*) is considered an intermediate state between death and glorification in heaven. It is a time of purification so that the souls of those who die in the state of grace can be readied for heaven. Ancient practices of praying for the dead were developed in the Roman Catholic tradition through several church councils over the centuries. After death, in this view, one is judged for eternal destiny in heaven or hell. If one's soul is not fully free from sin, and thus not ready for heaven, but is not to be consigned to hell, a period of purification is necessary. These persons are thus assured of salvation but must undergo this period in purgatory so that they can achieve the holiness they need to be fit for heaven.

The sixteenth-century Protestant reformers rejected both prayers for the dead and purgatory as being unbiblical. The kickoff of the Reformation was when Martin Luther (1483–1546) objected to the Roman Catholic Church's sale of indulgences, which could be bought by the living to reduce the number of years one's departed loved ones would have to spend in purgatory. In the Roman Catholic view, almsgiving and works of penance by those on earth on behalf of the departed can help those in purgatory.

The emphasis of the Reformers was on salvation by God's grace through faith in Jesus Christ. This faith is personal and leads the Christian to do good works as an expression or response in faith. Works themselves do not enable one to merit heaven after death. When death occurs, those who are saved by faith experience the resurrection of the body and eternal life in heaven. No intermediate state such as purgatory, or a process of purification, or prayers on behalf of the deceased have an effect or standing in relation to one's salvation. After physical death, the fullness of salvation is experienced directly without an intervening intermediate state. Calvin rejected the idea of soul sleep, that one's soul is in a state of dormancy between the time of death and the future resurrection. The Reformed tradition has rejected purgatory as being "opposed to the Christian faith" (*BC* 5.238).

89. What will heaven be like?

We do not know. Biblical people believed the cosmos was three-tiered: earth was at the center; heaven, the abode of God, was "on high" (Ps. 92:8); the underworld (or Sheol), the place of the dead, was below. Over all was God, who was thought to be present everywhere (Ps. 139:8; Matt. 6:9).

The theological reality of heaven is as the future, eternal dwelling place of the saints of God who receive salvation in Jesus Christ. Heaven is from where Christ descended (John 6:38) and to where he ascended to be with God the Father (Acts 1:10–11; Eph. 1:20). Heaven becomes the eternal home of God's righteous people in Christ (John 14:2–4; 2 Cor. 5:1; Eph. 2:6; Rev. 11:12).

The ultimate blessedness of eternity in God's presence is captured in the Westminster Larger Catechism, which says the righteous "shall be received into heaven, where they shall be fully and forever freed from all sin and misery; filled with inconceivable joy; made perfectly holy and happy both in body and soul, in the company of innumerable saints and angels, but especially in the immediate vision and fruition of God the Father, of our Lord Jesus Christ, and of the Holy Spirit, to all eternity" (*BC* 7.200).

In our present human condition, we cannot fathom the glories of eternity in the presence of God, everlasting praise, gold abounding—all in a "new heaven and new earth" (Rev. 21:1). The contrast between this reality and our own is incomprehensible. Imagine:

> "He will wipe every tear from their eyes.
> Death shall be no more;
> mourning and crying and pain will be no more."
> (Rev. 21:4)

"Glorification" is the theological term for the eternal salvation of those in the "book of life" (Rev. 21:27), now made complete in heaven. The Word who "lived among us" in Jesus Christ (John 1:14) is worshiped as the Lamb (Rev. 19:7) and as the conqueror of all sin and evil (Rev. 18). Now, ultimately,

> "the home of God is among mortals.
> He will dwell with them as their God;
> they will be his peoples."
> (Rev. 21:3)

> "Hallelujah!
> For the Lord our God
> the Almighty reigns."
> (Rev. 19:6)

90. What will hell be like?

A favorite reading for high school American literature classes has been Jonathan Edwards's (1703–1758) famous sermon "Sinners in the Hands of an Angry God." It has formed many people's pictures of hell. A sinner, like a spider, is said to be held by God over the pit of hell and may be dropped into that pit anytime.

Graphic images from some Reformed confessions also convey this: "But the unbelievers and ungodly will descend with the devils into hell to burn forever and never to be redeemed from torments (Matt. 25:46)" (*BC* 5.074). Or, "the souls of the wicked are cast into hell, where they remain in torments and utter darkness, reserved to the judgment of the great day" (Luke 16:23; *BC* 6.177; cf. 6.181).

The Old Testament sees the place of the dead as "Sheol," located somewhere beneath the earth (Ps. 139:8; Isa. 14:9). All souls reside there. In the New Testament, the term *Gehenna* is translated as "hell." It refers literally to the garbage dump outside Jerusalem where an everlasting fire burned and symbolically to where those under divine judgment will reside (Matt. 5:22; 23:33; Mark 9:43–48) with Satan (Matt. 25:41; Rev. 19:20).

Hell represents an eternal separation from God, due to sin. Some take the biblical images literally, as in Edwards's sermon. But the theological focus of hell is on separation from "the favorable presence of God, and the glorious fellowship with Christ" (*BC* 7.199). Refusing true life from Christ in this life is "to choose the death which is separation from God" (*BC* 9.11).

While "hell" points to the reality of future judgment, it is also a present word. Rejecting God's will and way here and now ruptures our relationship with God and others (sin). It leads ultimately to death (Rom. 6:23; Jer. 23:8). To live the lie that we can manage just fine without God endangers us eternally. To oppose God by lives of self-interest and self-absorption puts us in danger of separation that will not be overcome (Luke 16:19–31).

We do not know what hell will be like. We do know "hell" points us now toward Jesus Christ, in whom God's reconciliation prevails over sin and evil (Rev. 20).

91. Will all people be saved?

This question has been debated through the history of the church. Consistently, the church has affirmed human destiny will be either heaven or hell. Yet there have been different opinions about how best to understand this view.

Presbyterians historically have seen salvation as given to God's elect through the gift of faith in Jesus Christ. This is "election" or "predestination." Some in the Reformed tradition have argued for "double predestination," that some are foreordained to eternal death and others to eternal life, "before the foundation of the world" (Eph. 1:4). Other Reformed theologians have emphasized God's election to salvation and the "passing over" of those in their sin so they receive the due consequences of sin. "Universalism" is the view that all people will be saved. Although a historic view, it has always been a minority position. If God is love (1 John 4:16) and God "desires everyone to be saved" (1 Tim. 2:4), then God's grace will envelope the whole creation and all people will come to salvation. Some also see God's grace as operative after death, a "divine perseverance," so there are postdeath opportunities to respond to the gospel.

While we wonder about this question, we realize we do not have to decide about it, since this is God's decision and not ours. We are to proclaim the gospel of Jesus Christ as vigorously and persuasively as possible even when it appears to be "foolishness," while in reality it is "the power of God" (1 Cor. 1:18). God is free to choose whom to save and to save whomever by whatever means God desires. God's free grace is given according to God's will.

Our prayers should be for all people to know "the only true God" and Jesus Christ whom God has sent (John 17:3). If it is possible for all to be saved, what Christian would not want this to be so? If we do not, where is our love? As the Second Helvetic Confession suggests, "We must hope well of all, and not rashly judge any [person] to be a reprobate" (*BC* 5.055). In the end, God is "above all and through all and in all" (Eph. 4:6).

For Further Reading

Angell, James W. *How to Spell Presbyterian*. Newly rev. ed. Louisville, KY: Geneva Press, 2002.

Being Reformed: Faith Seeking Understanding. Adult Curriculum. Congregational Ministries Publishing. Presbyterian Church (U.S.A.). http://www.pcusa.org/beingreformed.

Calvin, John. *Institutes of the Christian Religion*. Ed. John T. McNeill. Trans. Ford Lewis Battles. Library of Christian Classics. 2 vols. Philadelphia: Westminster Press, 1960.

The Constitution of the Presbyterian Church (U.S.A.). Part I, *Book of Confessions*. Louisville, KY: Office of the General Assembly, 2002.

Gerstner, John H. *Theology for Everyman*. Chicago: Moody Press, 1965.

Guthrie, Shirley C., Jr. *Always Being Reformed: Faith for a Fragmented World*. 2nd ed. Louisville, KY: Westminster John Knox Press, 2008.

————. *Christian Doctrine*. Rev. ed. Louisville, KY: Westminster John Knox Press, 1994.

Johnson, Earl S., Jr. *Witness without Parallel: Eight Biblical Texts That Make Us Presbyterian*. Louisville, KY: Geneva Press, 2003.

Leitch, Addison H. *A Layman's Guide to Presbyterian Beliefs*. Grand Rapids: Zondervan, 1967.

Leith, John H. *Introduction to the Reformed Tradition: A Way of Being the Christian Community*. Atlanta: John Knox Press, 1980.

Lingle, Walter L., and John W. Kuykendall. *Presbyterians: Their History and Beliefs*. 4th rev. ed. Atlanta: John Knox Press, 1978.

McKim, Donald K., ed. *Calvin's* Institutes: *Abridged Edition*. Louisville, KY: Westminster John Knox Press, 2001.

————. *Introducing the Reformed Faith: Biblical Revelation, Christian Tradition, Contemporary Significance*. Louisville, KY: Westminster John Knox Press, 2001.

————. *Presbyterian Beliefs: A Brief Introduction*. Louisville, KY: Geneva Press, 2003.

————. *Presbyterian Questions, Presbyterian Answers*. Louisville, KY: Geneva Press, 2003.

————, ed. *The Westminster Handbook to Reformed Theology*. Louisville, KY: Westminster John Knox Press, 2001.

Plunkett, Stephen W. *This We Believe: Eight Truths Presbyterians Affirm*. Louisville, KY: Westminster John Knox Press, 2002.

The Presbyterian Leader. Presbyterian Publishing Corporation. http://www.thepresbyterianleader.com.

Rogers, Jack. *Presbyterian Creeds: A Guide to the* Book of Confessions. Louisville, KY: Westminster John Knox Press, 1991.

————. *Reading the Bible and the Confessions: The Presbyterian Way*. Louisville, KY: Westminster John Knox Press, 1999.

Rohls, Jan. *Reformed Confessions: Theology from Zurich to Barmen*. Trans. John Hoffmeyer. Columbia Series in Reformed Theology. Louisville, KY: Westminster John Knox Press, 1998.

Weeks, Louis B. *The Presbyterian Source: Bible Words That Shape a Faith*. Louisville, KY: Westminster/John Knox Press, 1990.

————. *To Be a Presbyterian*. Rev. ed. Louisville, KY: Geneva Press, 2010.

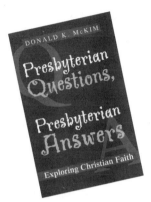

My previous *Presbyterian Questions, Presbyterian Answers: Exploring Christian Faith* (Louisville: Geneva Press, 2003) considered other questions and answers for Presbyterians. It is a supplement to the present volume and can be used in the same way as this book for group and individual study.

Contents

7 Salvation

8 Church

9 Worship